The Healthy Lifestyle
DIET COOKBOOK

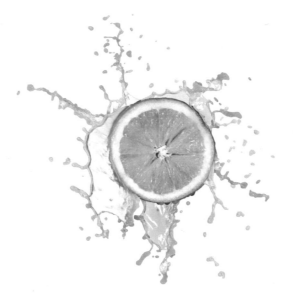

The Healthy Lifestyle
DIET COOKBOOK

Sarah Flower

SPRING HILL

Published by Spring Hill, an imprint of How To Books Ltd.
Spring Hill House, Spring Hill Road
Begbroke, Oxford OX5 1RX
United Kingdom
Tel: (01865) 375794
Fax: (01865) 379162
info@howtobooks.co.uk
www.howtobooks.co.uk

First published 2012

How To Books greatly reduce the carbon footprint of their books by sourcing their
typesetting and printing in the UK.

British Library Cataloguing in Publication Data
A catalogue record of this book is available from the British Library.

ISBN: 978 1 905862 74 0

Produced for How To Books by Deer Park Productions, Tavistock, Devon
Designed and typeset by Mousemat Design Ltd
Printed and bound by in Great Britain by Bell & Bain Ltd, Glasgow

NOTE: The material contained in this book is set out in good faith for general guidance
and no liability can be accepted for loss or expense incurred as a result of relying in
particular circumstances on statements made in the book. Laws and regulations are
complex and liable to change, and readers should check the current position with relevant
authorities before making personal arrangements.

Contents

Introduction

I have been looking forward to writing a healthy eating cookbook. One of my previous books, *Eat Well, Spend Less* combined advice for money saving with healthier cooking choices. This book is all about long-term, lifestyle health for the whole family.

I tried to resist the word 'diet', much preferring to refer to this way of eating as a healthy lifestyle regime, but really no other word conveys the same message. So here it is, *The Healthy Lifestyle Diet Cookbook*. If you adopt the food swaps and recipes suggested you will most likely lose weight, but you will also become healthier and have more energy. This book is designed to be a family cookbook so the whole family can enjoy healthy food – and as such, I have included many family favourites, all with a healthy twist.

This book does not count calories, so those looking for a calorie count in each recipe will be disappointed. The reason? It is all about adopting a healthier lifestyle diet for the whole family – no calorie counting or fad rules and regulations: just real, honest food. My only concession to 'diet' food is opting for low-fat versions of our common foods (such as crème fraîche, yoghurt, cheese, skimmed milk), but I want to encourage you to eat lots more good fats – such as oily fish, good oils, nuts and seeds. These may have calorie-counting experts jumping up and down with frustration but we need oil in our diet – it is crucial for good health inside and out, meaning that those who advocate a strict low-fat diet will not only suffer more from ill health, they will also start to go wrinkly sooner!

One of the other drawbacks of low-fat diets is how people concentrate so much on things being low fat, they forget to look at what else is going on in the diet. Low-fat diets can often be high in carbohydrates (and I'm talking the bad carbs: white flour, sugar, white pasta etc.). They are often lower in fibre and wholegrain and always lacking in essential fatty acids. I wanted to put together a healthy eating plan offering a balance of good wholesome food.

I recommend using natural sugar substitutes such as Xylitol, Sweet Freedom or Stevia more frequently, all of which are explained in Chapter 1: 'Food Swaps for Health'. When I was growing up, the only negative thing we were taught about sugar was its power to rot our teeth, but there are much more sinister health issues to deal with. Like many nutritionists, I believe there is a very strong link between obesity and our consumption of sugary foods. These kinds of foods may initially give you a burst of energy, but they will leave you with a low blood sugar slump (often experienced mid-afternoon when you are wanting to grab the nearest chocolate bar!). Excess sugar can lead to weight gain, but also can ultimately lead to diabetes. If you are overweight, it is estimated that you are over 100

> **Did you know?**
> 250 million people worldwide are affected by diabetes. This is predicted to rise to 350 million in 2025.

times more likely to suffer from diabetes.

High sugar levels convert to glucose and raise blood sugar levels. To stabilise this and remove dangerous glucose from the bloodstream, our bodies produce insulin. However, the glucose isn't broken down and excreted as we may hope; instead it is converted to fat. Sadly, not only do our bodies convert excess glucose into fat, the fat already stored in our bodies may not break down – which is why many people find it hard to shift weight, especially when they are not addressing their sugar intake.

I won't get too technical, but please trust me on this: if you only take one thing from this book it is to reduce your sugar consumption. I know Xylitol and Stevia are more expensive than sugar, but the health benefits are huge. I have also seen positive results from low glycemic index (GI) diets, so you will see this come up occasionally throughout the book, though this is not a low GI diet book.

Somes recipes suggest gluten-free/wheat-free options. Whether or not you are on a gluten/wheat-free diet, you may want to consider using a gluten/wheat-free alternative – many people can suffer from bloating and digestive problems caused by wheat without actually being wheat or gluten intolerant. There are so many wheat-free options available now for bread, pasta and flours – it really is an easy food swap.

I recommend taking the time to read the informative chapters at the beginning of the book – they are there to help and support you on your journey towards better health. They will help you understand why I am recommending certain food swaps, what to have in your store-cupboard and even offer tips on how to avoid grabbing the nearest chocolate bar when you are feeling emotional.

Here is a quick summary of how to maintain a healthy lifestyle diet.

- As a general rule of thumb, try to eat at least three oily fish main meals a week and two vegetarian. Try to eat meat no more than two or three times a week and opt for clean, lean meats.
- Eat plenty of fresh fruit and vegetables.
- Always opt for wholegrain rather than 'white' refined.
- Choose pulses and beans to help bulk meals out, keeping you fuller for longer.
- Avoid processed foods – especially junk food.
- Avoid frying – especially deep fat!
- Eat plenty of good fats: oily fish, nuts, seeds and good oils. It will also help to take a good quality fish oil supplement daily, such as krill oil.
- Limit salt and sugar intake.
- Drink plenty of water.
- Avoid too much caffeine and alcohol.
- Get moving – exercise for at least 15–20 minutes a day.

I always welcome emails from readers and look forward to any feedback on how you get on with this book. I will be updating new recipes and ideas on my blog, so keep a look out. Visit my website: www.sarahflower.co.uk or follow me on twitter: MsSarahFlower. If you have enjoyed this book, I hope you will recommend it to others.

Good luck and good health!

Sarah xx

Conversion charts

This book provides metric measurements, but those who still prefer Imperial, or who want to use US measures, can use these conversions.

Liquids		
Metric	Imperial	US cups
5ml	1 tsp	1 tsp
15ml	1 tbsp	1 tbsp
50ml	2fl oz	3 tbsp
60ml	2½ fl oz	¼ cup
75ml	3fl oz	⅓ cup
100ml	4fl oz	scant ½ cup
125ml	4½ fl oz	½ cup
150ml	5fl oz	⅔ cup
200ml	7fl oz	scant 1 cup
250ml	10fl oz	1 cup
300ml	½pt	1¼ cups
350ml	12fl oz	1⅓ cups
400ml	¾pt	1½ cups
500ml	20fl oz	2 cups
600ml	1pt	2½ cups

Weight	
Metric	Imperial
25g	1oz
50g	2oz
75g	3oz
100g	4oz
150g	5oz
175g	6oz
200g	7oz
225g	8oz
250g	9oz
300g	10oz
350g	12oz
400g	14oz
450g	1lb

Measurements	
Metric	Imperial
5cm	2in
10cm	4in
13cm	5in
15cm	6in
18cm	7in
20cm	8in
25cm	10in
30cm	12in

Oven temperatures	
Metric	Imperial
110°C	225°F
120°C	250°F
140°C	275°F
150°C	300°F
160°C	325°F
180°C	350°F
190°C	375°F
200°C	400°F
220°C	425°F
230°C	450°F
240°C	475°F

Chapter 1
Food swaps for health

This chapter details the everyday items you can swap for a healthier alternative, helping you to achieve a healthier lifestyle without noticing too much change.

Sugar

Swap for: Xylitol, Sweet Freedom, Stevia or fruit

I would urge anyone wanting to lose weight or maintain a healthier lifestyle to try to substitute sugar wherever possible. Do not use artificial sweeteners – I personally have concerns about the high chemical content of artificial sweeteners and there are mounting health concerns surrounding aspartame. Instead, opt for natural sweeteners. As your tastes change, you will start to notice and enjoy the natural sweetness from fruits and not be so reliant on excessive sugar hits. Reducing sugar will help lower your blood sugar and help prevent gradual weight gain. People have reported a reduction in sugar cravings by taking a daily supplement of chromium as it helps balance blood sugar.

Xylitol

This is a natural sugar alternative that looks, feels and tastes just like sugar, but it has 45% less calories, 75% less available carbohydrates, a GI value of just 7 and actively promotes healthy teeth. It is also ideal for diabetics. It is available from health food stores and some leading supermarkets under the name Total Sweet. You can also buy Xylitol from online health companies such as Higher Nature.

Sweet Freedom natural sweetness – Original & Dark

These versatile syrup based alternatives to white and brown sugar contain just three ingredients: apples, grapes and carob, and nothing else! Benefits include; 25% fewer calories than sugar plus use 25% less gram for gram to achieve the same sweetness. They also have a low GL (glycaemic load) meaning they won't cause blood sugar and energy highs and lows. These sweeteners are great for the whole family, from dieters to diabetics alike and kids love the taste. They are now available from the sugar shelf in supermarkets and also in health food shops.

Stevia

The stevia leaf contains numerous phytonutrients and trace minerals and is diabetic safe. The leaves of stevia contain glycosides, the sweetening power of which is between 250 and 400 times their equivalent in sugar. It has been available worldwide for many years but was only launched in the UK in December 2011. The leading brandnames in the UK are Pure Via™, Truvia® and

La Maison Du Stevia. You will use much less stevia than sugar so be aware and adjust recipes to suit your palate. Some companies are launching sugars made with half stevia, half sugar, so always read the label to know what you are buying.

Salt

Swap for: *natural herbs and spices or Solo® Low Sodium Sea Salt*
Most people consume far too much salt (sodium) in their diets. Your maximum daily allowance is 6g. This is just over 1 teaspoon per day, so keep that in mind when you randomly throw salt in your cooking or pile it over your food. Remember that most junk or processed foods contain a lot of salt (sodium), so in order to cut down, opt for home-cooked. Excess salt leads to high blood pressure, some cancers, including stomach cancer, osteoporosis and heart disease. If you would like to start reducing your salt gradually, opt for something like Solo® Low Sodium Sea Salt, which has 66% less sodium than table, rock and sea salt and is also packed with great minerals such as potassium and magnesium.

Oil

Swap for: *seeded oils such as flax oil, oily fish and seeds*
As much as the media like to push fat-free diets, we do need to have 'good' fats/oils in our diet for optimum health. Swapping vegetable oil for olive oil is a good start, giving you omega-9, but the real benefits come when you start to use oils rich in omega-3, such as flax oil. You can only use flax oil cold (as heating destroys the nutrients), so why not swap olive oil for flax oil when making a dressing, a cold dip such as hummus, or a salsa. You can get omega-3 in your diet by eating oily fish such as mackerel, sardines, salmon and fresh tuna but also from walnuts, Brazil nuts, hazelnuts, pecans, sesame seeds and rapeseed oil. You gain omega-6 from sunflower, pumpkin and sesame seeds, evening primrose, safflower and soya oils. The real baddies are trans fats, most commonly described in product labelling as hydrogenated fats. You will find these in most processed or junk foods – always read the labels and try to avoid.

Milk

Swap for: *skimmed milk or soya milk*
We all know we should stop opting for full-fat milk. Instead use skimmed milk, which actually contains more calcium than full-fat milk. You could also try soya milk (this is fine for cooking most things, though it does curdle in coffee). Rice and oat milk are also available, though they are more expensive options.

Cream

Swap for: low-fat crème fraîche, 0% fat Greek yoghurt, low-fat cream cheese or quark

Cream is used in many recipes or to accompany desserts. Instead opt for low-fat crème fraîche, low-fat natural yoghurt (I use Total 0% in cooking), low-fat cream cheese or, the lowest fat option, quark. Quark can taste a bit odd on its own so if you are using it to accompany a dessert instead of cream, mix it with a little vanilla essence and some low-fat crème fraîche. For added sweetness, you could stir in a little Sweet Freedom syrup.

Cheese

Swap for: Nutritional Yeast Flakes, low-fat cheese

Many of us love cheese, but did you know you can cut down on the amount you use for things like cheese sauces or even cheesy scrambled eggs by using a product called Nutritional Yeast Flakes. These flakes are more commonly used by vegans who want the cheesy flavour without the dairy, but they can of course be used by anyone. If you add a few tablespoons to a cheese sauce, before you add the cheese, you can reduce by at least half the amount of cheese you need to use. *Plus*, Nutritional Yeast Flakes are packed with B vitamins. Remember, if you love cheese, swap to a low-fat version – there are now many great tasting options on the market. Also, if you are using cheddar in cooking, opt for mature cheddar as you need less to create the flavour.

Ice-cream

Swap for: frozen yoghurt or frozen smoothies

I know everyone loves ice-cream, but it is not great for our health. Why not try frozen yoghurt or make your own smoothies (see Chapter 4) and freeze them – much healthier. Sorbets are very light and cleansing on the palate but can be very high in sugar (unless you follow my Raspberry Sorbet recipe in Chapter 11).

Chocolate

Swap for: dark chocolate (at least 70% cocoa solids)

We all love chocolate, but avoid the extra sweet confectionary made with dairy milk. For those serious about health, opt instead for dark chocolate – ideally at least 70% cocoa content. Dark chocolate contains a high level of antioxidants. These flavonoids can help prevent heart disease, cell damage and have even been linked to helping prevent cancer. Dark chocolate has been shown to

stimulate the production of endorphins. It has also been shown to help with minor depression as it contains serotonin – a natural anti-depressent. But before you rush off to eat loads of chocolate, remember that it has to be a pure source of dark chocolate and everything in moderation!

A little goes a long way and, yes, you will soon adjust to the taste and wonder how you could have ever eaten that sickly sweet Mars® bar. I recommend Willie Harcourt's Pure Cacao (£5.99 from Waitrose or visit www.williescacao.com), which is great in savoury and sweet recipes. I am a huge fan, even more so as it is actually a very healthy product – chocolate and healthy … my type of food!

Refined carbohydrates

Swap for: wholegrains, seeds, nuts, and cereals

One of the biggest problems in many of our diets is the high level of refined carbohydrates, which basically means all the white stuff – sugar, flour, pasta, bread, biscuits and cakes, the list is endless. These refined carbohydrates convert to glucose, raising your blood sugar levels (and contributing to an increased risk of diabetes). If an excessive amount of carbohydrates are consumed and not 'burned' off, they are converted into fat. Instead, swap for complex carbohydrates, which basically means the foods that haven't been processed, such as wholewheat pasta, brown flour, wholegrains, cereals, nuts and seeds. These foods contain more nutrients and don't have the same negative effect as refined carbohydrates.

Crisps

Swap for: popcorn, peanuts, savoury Nairn's Oatcakes

Crisps can be high in fat and salt and contain very little nutrients. If you fancy a savoury snack, why not try popping your own popcorn. Corn kernels are cheap to buy and take just minutes to 'pop'. Kids also love watching them expand and pop in the pan. See the great recipe for Chocolate Popcorn in Chapter 11. Peanuts have a low GI which means they don't raise your blood sugar levels, but instead give you even, slowly released energy. Buy salt-free peanuts and add to things like salads to help keep you feeling fuller for longer. If you are craving a savoury snack, eat a few Nairn's Oatcakes – they are also low GI. Please forget about diving in for the rice cakes thinking you are choosing an excellent snack. They are high GI and don't really give you much goodness. Instead choose a wholesome snack or a handful of peanuts, a bowl of cherries or a handful of seeds.

Fizzy drinks

Swap for: water, fresh juices, green tea

Fizzy drinks contain high levels of sugar and caffeine and very little nutrients. Many professionals consider the high consumption of fizzy drinks to be one of the biggest causes of obesity, Type 2 diabetes and dental problems. The high consumption of 'diet' fizzy drinks has also been linked, because of the artificial sweetener, to mental health problems. Most fizzy drinks also contain phosphoric acid, which can interfere with the body's ability to utilise calcium, leading to problems such as osteoporosis. The caffeine and cocktail of chemicals in fizzy drinks can also upset your natural stomach acid balance, leading to gastrointestinal problems.

Caffeine

Swap for: green coffee, dandelion coffee, green tea, herbal teas or water!

We are becoming increasingly reliant on caffeine, believing it is going to give us a mental or physical boost to help us through the day. However, caffeine can play havoc with an already compromised adrenal system – add to the mix a stressed lifestyle where you eat on the run and often grab sugary snacks to get you through the day and the result is a recipe for serious health problems. Cut down your dependency on caffeine – you may get a headache for the first few days but do persevere.

Green coffee has been shown to aid weight loss, increase energy, detoxify, increase memory and some even claim improvement of skin problems. You can buy it in powder form (just like an instant coffee) or in capsules. Green tea contains antioxidants called catechins, and has been shown to aid health, including in some research into cancer, diabetes, stroke and heart disease.

Did you know?

Green tea is rich in polyphenols which have been shown to help fight against many cancers including, breast, lung, stomach, throat and colon cancer. It also helps burn fat and can speed up your metabolism, making it a perfect choice for those wanting to aid weight loss.

Chapter 2
Store cupboard essentials

This chapter will help you sort out your store cupboards, so that you are ready for healthy eating and for preparing the recipes that follow. Most of the recipes in this book use everyday items but some are a little more unique, such as the sugar replacement (see Chapter 1 for more information).

Fridge
- Pure or low-fat margarine
- Quark
- Fat-free natural yoghurt
- Fat-free greek yoghurt
- Low-fat crème fraîche
- Low-fat cheese (mature cheddar, parmesan, feta)
- Skimmed milk
- Eggs
- Fresh fruit and vegetables
- Lean meat
- Oily fish (salmon, mackerel, tuna, herring, trout)

Cooking basics
- Olive oil (use spray when cooking)
- Flax oil or Good Oil (this is a pure natural oil made from cold-pressed hemp seed and is very rich in omega 3, 6 and 9)
- Balsamic vinegar
- White wine vinegar
- Wholegrain mustard
- Black pepper
- Sea salt (or low sodium salt)

Dry store
- Porridge oats
- Wholemeal plain flour
- Wholemeal self-raising flour
- Doves Farm Gluten Free Self-Raising Flour

- Baking powder (gluten-free is available)
- Semolina (for roast potatoes!)
- Cornflour
- Xylitol
- Stevia
- Sweet Freedom Natural Sweetness – Original and Dark
- Low salt stock
- Nutritional yeast flakes
- Popcorn kernels (for popping)
- Dried apricots
- Barley
- Nairn's Oatcakes

Pulses and beans
- Red lentils
- Brown lentils
- Puy lentils
- Chickpeas
- Red kidney beans
- Mixed beans
- Borlotti beans (great for digestion)
- Haricot beans
- Butter beans
- Baked beans (opt for low salt, low sugar)
- Split peas

Pasta and rice
- Wholemeal pasta and spaghetti
- Gluten-free pasta and spaghetti (I use rice and vegetable pasta)
- Basmati rice
- Brown rice

Nuts and seeds
- Mixed seeds
- Sunflower seeds
- Pumpkin seeds
- Peanuts (buy salt-free)
- Walnuts

- Almonds
- Cashew

Bread

- Wholemeal, wholewheat, nutty, seeded bread
- Rye bread
- Pumpernickel bread
- Tortilla
- Wholemeal pitta bread
- Gluten-free bread

Herbs and spices

A basic spice rack will provide you with most of the spices used in this book. But herbs are

unbeatable when used fresh. If you have a windowsill or garden, you can grow your own herbs. Don't buy them fresh from the supermarket as you may be paying a premium. If you can't grow your own, or if the herbs you need to use are out of season, a great product I have recently tried is frozen herbs. For the same price as fresh, you can buy a large container of freshly frozen herbs that can last you months and offer a superior taste over dried varieties.

- Paprika – This rich red spice has a very delicate flavour, unless you buy hot paprika which tastes quite different! I use it on my roast potatoes and also in soups and casseroles, and even sprinkled on cheese on toast.

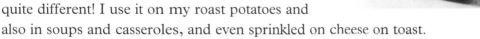

- Garam masala – A blend of herbs and spices traditionally used in Indian cookery.
- Sweet curry powder – This has a mild curry flavour which is perfect for a child's dahl or in a quick and easy curry sauce to have with your potato wedges.
- Curry paste – I love curry paste: it can add an instant zing to a meal. I make my own and store it in the fridge or freeze into ice cube trays. Try the Simple Chicken Curry recipe in Chapter 8.
- Chilli powder or freeze-dried chillis – Great for adding a bit of spice to your dishes. Try mixing some chilli powder with grated cheese before toasting – delicious! I grow my own chilli plants in the summer and if I have any leftover chillis I bottle them in oil or freeze them whole until I need them.
- Ground cinnamon – I love cinnamon, especially in biscuits, apple cakes or apple pies. I use cinnamon powder as I find the sticks too expensive and to be honest, too much hassle.

- Ground coriander – This is lovely in savoury dishes, but I also use it in cakes as it has a surprising flavour.
- Ground ginger – Don't mistake this for fresh ginger as they taste quite different. Ground ginger is good in savoury dishes and excellent for baking.
- Nutmeg – I have a few whole nutmegs in a jar and use a fine grater to add a bit of nutmeg magic to my food. Great in baking, but also very comforting sprinkled on milky drinks and puddings.
- Mixed spice – Optional, but good if you love baking.
- Turmeric – Some call this the poor man's saffron, but nutritionally, it is a very good product. Add to savoury dishes or use to colour rice that lovely vibrant yellow.
- Mixed herbs – This is a good safe option for newbie cooks. Add to savoury dishes, salad dressing and even sprinkle on pizzas if you don't have any oregano.
- Dried bay leaves – Don't underestimate a bay leaf: they can really add life to a savoury dish, particularly soups.

Chapter 3
Eat yourself healthy

Healthy eating is very simply going back to basics. If you use fresh ingredients for at least 80% of your diet, you really will be achieving better health. It is common sense. Food that has been put together in a factory is going to contain fewer nutrients than pure food. Treat your food with respect. Your health is so important and it is only when we get older that we really appreciate this.

My biggest concern is for our children. Without the good, healthy foundations in place, they are likely to develop ill health far quicker than other generations. According to the Department of Health, direct costs caused by obesity are estimated to be £4.2 billion per year and forecast to more than double by 2050 if we carry on as we are. Parents are getting accustomed to seeing obese children so they are becoming less aware of their own child's weight problems. A study by Peninsula Medical School in Plymouth revealed that three-quarters of parents failed to recognise their child was overweight. Thirty-three per cent of mums and 57 percent of dads considered their child's weight to be 'about right' when, in fact, they were obese.

> Good news for those wanting to lose weight. Losing just 10% of your body weight can also slash your cholesterol by 10% and reduce your risk of diabetes.

Are you getting enough?
We all need to eat at least five portions of fruit and vegetables a day. We have seen the government campaign but do we really understand what it means and why it is so important? I did a workshop at a primary school recently and I was horrified to discover that the teacher believed five a day was a maximum! It is actually the minimum we should consume. Please ignore the marketing ploys to encourage you to buy junk food in order to get your five a day. There really is no way a chewy bar contains the same nutrients and phytonutrients as a fruit or vegetable.

> Did you know?
> Potatoes do not count as part of your five a day.

What is a portion?
- 2 small fruits, such as satsuma, kiwi or plum
- 1 medium fruit, such as apple, pear, orange or banana
- Half a large fruit, such as melon, grapefruit or pineapple
- 30g of dried fruit
- 4 heaped tbsp of green vegetables
- 3 heaped tbsp of cooked vegetables such as carrots or peas
- 3 heaped tbsp of pulses or beans (baked beans do count!)

- 150ml of unsweetened fruit or vegetable juice (further glasses of juice don't count toward your total five a day)
- 100% fruit or vegetable smoothies count as 2 portions

Why do we need a minimum of five a day?

Fruit and vegetables contain health-busting vitamins and minerals as well as essential phytonutrients which help protect you from diseases such as cancer and heart disease. They contain fibre which can help keep your bowel healthy and happy, and they also help create a balanced diet.

Portion sizes

When serving food, we tend to load a plate and overeat. Try using a smaller plate and you will soon be cutting down without really noticing. Use the same principle when feeding your children – they often feel intimidated by an overloaded plate. Far better to give them less and enjoy hearing them ask for more, rather than watch them struggle with a large meal.

Did you know?
Using smaller plates may reduce your calorie intake by up to 22 per cent.

Chew your food

Digestion starts when the food enters your mouth and chewing is a vital part of our digestive process. Chew your food slowly and enjoy the taste of your food. Giving yourself time to eat will allow you to hear your body start telling you when you are full. If you shovel in the food quickly you will ignore this signal.

Sit at a table, not in front of the TV

This is not about etiquette. Your digestion will work better if you are sitting comfortably at a table, plus your attention will be on your food. Paul McKenna ran an interesting experiment by feeding unsuspecting cinema goers stale popcorn. No one noticed what it tasted like as they were too busy watching the film, and they all finished their large pots. The idea is conscious eating – if you are aware of every mouthful, you are less likely to make bad food choices, less likely to binge and more likely to listen to your body when it tells you it's full.

Get active

Dump the remote, hide the car keys, and do all you can to keep moving. Not only are you burning calories, you're also increasing your heart-rate, expanding your lungs and moving your muscles. Try to be more active during the day as a slow metabolism holds on to weight. If you exercise in the hour prior to eating, your metabolic rate is higher, which means that any calories taken in will be burnt off quicker. Activity will not only help you shed pounds, it will also help strengthen your heart. Aim for at least 20 minutes a day. Try swimming, walking, cycling or even join a dancing class. Whatever you choose make sure you have fun.

Get hydrated

Many people confuse thirst signals for hunger pangs. Drink plenty of water (not fizzy drinks, tea or coffee!). This will help re-hydrate you and will also keep hunger and headaches at bay. Dehydration also causes bad breath.

Ditch the frying pan

Grill or oven-bake instead of frying your foods. If you love chips, try baking potato wedges coated with paprika and sprayed with olive oil for a healthier option. I fill a spray container with light olive oil ready to spray food or pans, as this works well and reduces the oil content. You can buy sprays of olive oil in the supermarket (I found the 1 Cal sprays to be flavourless). Lakeland sell a spray container you can use to put your favourite olive oil in.

Colour therapy

You can tell at a glance whether a meal is healthy or not. Healthy food is full of colour and vibrancy. Junk food is biscuit coloured. Fill your plate with a variety of colours for a healthy and nutritious meal. You can choose your foods by their colour – for example, for side vegetables, you could opt for green cabbage, vibrant orange carrots and yellow sweetcorn. Get creative with your food colour palate.

Don't skip meals

Eat three nourishing meals a day. It is a complete myth that you will lose weight if you skip meals. All you will achieve is a slump in your blood sugar levels, headaches and general feeling of grottiness … all the more reason to grab the nearest chocolate bar and wallow in self-pity. Instead, eat more, but choose your food with care. Pack all your meals with nutritious wholegrains to avoid sugar slumps and cravings. Fill your diet with fruits, vegetables and wholegrains; there is no excuse, even when losing weight, to go hungry.

Smile!

Smiling and laughing increases the production of your feel-good endorphins. Not only will you feel better and more positive, but those around you will also benefit as smiling is contagious.

Go green

Ditch the caffeine and opt for the healthier substitutes. Start by switching to decaffeinated teas and coffees, but for ultimate health, cut down or ditch them altogether. Green tea, for example, is packed with powerful antioxidants which can help lower cholesterol, boost your immune system and lower blood pressure.

Cut the fizz

Fizzy drinks are packed with sugars and chemicals – even diet/sugar-free drinks are bad for you. If you like the fizz, try sparkling water mixed with fruit juice or natural cordial or, even better, a slice of lemon.

Avoid fast food

Fast food, junk food, processed food – they are all the same thing. They are packed with unhealthy fats, salts, sugars, chemicals and very little nutrients. They also cost more than home-cooked meals. So why do they account for approximately 70–80 per cent of the average family food shopping trolley? Change your processed food habit and opt for easy to make, home-cooked meals.

Time for you

Step out of the rat race and find some time in your busy life. Set aside some time every day just for you, even if it's for only five minutes. This could be reading, relaxing, a pampering session or just enjoying your favourite hobby. It may sound like a simple thing to do, but how often do you actually have time to yourself?

Respect your food

Learn to treat your food with respect and to get the most out of it. Food processing and cooking can destroy nutrients. Therefore buy fresh ingredients and make home-cooked meals. Think about how you can get the most benefit from your food.

Nutrients, particularly vitamins, are lost when you boil your vegetables. Buy a steamer to ensure your cooked vegetables remain packed with nutrients. They will taste better too. Invest in a wok and stir fry to lock in flavours and nutrients. Slow cookers are also a great tool not just for convenience but also for making nutrient-rich soups, casseroles and one-pot meals. Raw foods are also good for you. Try salads, smoothies, juices or simply eating some fresh fruit or vegetable sticks.

Back to school

Hobbies can improve your mental and physical health. Learn to cook, exercise or even knit (known to lower blood pressure). It will also help build confidence and help you to make new friends.

Emotional health

One of the biggest reasons we overeat is due to emotional stress (the other big reason is boredom!). Be aware of your emotions. Vitamin B supplements and St John's Wort can help ease stress and depression. Unhealthy diets, particularly those high in processed foods, can upset your natural balance and can contribute to emotional health problems. Changing to a nutrient-rich diet, whilst adding some interim supplementation, should really help.

Look after your teeth

Good teeth help you look younger and healthier. Have regular check-ups with your dentist. Brush and floss your teeth twice a day to avoid gum disease – the major cause of losing your teeth. Some research suggests that flossing your teeth daily can help you live longer!

Sleep

Yes, sleep is one of the best health-promoting activities. Aim for a good eight hours sleep a night. During sleep your body maintains its own glucose and insulin levels as well as growth hormone levels, which is why you don't wake up during the night craving a tasty snack. Disturbed sleep not only makes you grumpy but can have a serious effect on your metabolism. Shift workers, particularly those who vary their shift patterns, can suffer more from weight fluctuations and mental health problems.

Teach your children well

This is the most important legacy you can ever leave your children. Teach them to enjoy, respect and know their food. Start them young by feeding them wholesome foods as soon as they are weaned. Children don't need specially formulated kids' foods, or tempting with cartoon characters. They just need to learn to love food for what it is. They will emulate their parents – so if you love good food, they will too.

Chapter 4
Breakfast like a king...

Breakfast really is the most important meal of the day. It is very true that your concentration and mental alertness are more sluggish if you skip this essential meal. People often comment that they struggle to lose weight, yet eat very little. Breakfast is usually the one meal they avoid in a bid to reduce calories, but this results in the body hanging onto body fat and a tendency for the dieter to start snacking on inappropriate options mid morning when the hunger pangs become too strong to avoid.

Porridge with Fresh Fruit

2

Porridge is one of the best breakfasts you can have but, please, resist the urge to sweeten it with sugar. If you prefer sweetened porridge, try Xylitol or Sweet Freedom Syrup. Choose a selection of fresh seasonal fruit, or you could opt for a compote of fruit made from frozen berries, sweetened with a little Sweet Freedom Syrup.

1. Prepare the fruit and place in a bowl. If you have removed the fruit from the fridge, try to leave it at room temperature for at least 20 minutes as this will enhance the flavours, especially of the strawberries.

2. Place the porridge oats in a saucepan. Cover with skimmed milk. Cook on a low/medium heat and stir continually. As it starts to thicken, add more milk until you reach the desired consistency.

3. Place the porridge in the bowls and place a generous spoonful of the fruit on the top.

4. If you like extra sweetness, drizzle a small amount of Sweet Freedom Syrup over the fruit. Serve immediately.

Did you know?
Oats help reduce cholesterol. They are also high energy.

Porridge with Spicy Fruit Compote

Ingredients:

6 ripe strawberries, quartered
Small handful of blueberries
1 nectarine, sliced
6–8 raspberries
60g porridge oats (or gluten-free)
150–250ml skimmed milk (or soya milk)
Drizzle of Sweet Freedom dark (optional)

Nutritional information:

Vegetarian, vegan, wheat free, gluten free, low sugar, low fat, good for your heart

Porridge with Spicy Fruit Compote

Ingredients:

100g prunes

100g figs

50g currants

50g raisins

350ml water

1 tbsp Xylitol or Sweet
Freedom Dark

1 cinnamon stick

4–6 whole cloves

1 orange, peeled and
sliced/segmented

Zest and juice of 1 orange

1 banana, sliced

100g porridge oats (or
gluten-free)

300ml skimmed milk (or
soya milk)

Nutritional information:

Vegetarian, vegan, wheat
free, gluten free, low
sugar, low fat, high
energy, good for your
heart, aids digestion

This compote can be made in advance and stored in the fridge –
just leave out the banana until you are preparing the dish to
serve. Use with porridge, natural yoghurt or as a dessert served
with a dollop of low-fat crème fraîche or quark.

1. Place the dried fruit in a saucepan with the water, xylitol or
syrup, cinnamon and cloves. Bring to the boil.

2. Add orange slices, zest and juice. Cover and cook on
low/medium heat for 15 minutes. Add more water if needed.
Remove the cinnamon stick and cloves. Store until needed or
place on a very low heat while you cook the porridge.

3. Place the porridge oats in a saucepan. Cover with skimmed
milk. Cook on a low/medium heat and stir continually. As it starts
to thicken, add more milk until you reach the desired consistency.

4. When ready to serve, reheat your fruit compote (if necessary)
and add the banana.
Place the porridge in the bowls and place a generous spoonful of
the compote on the top. Eat and enjoy!

Did you know?
Porridge can help lower cholesterol, keep you fuller for
longer and has even been shown to help prevent heart
disease. Oats are also great if you have lost your appetite
(eat little and often) or suffer from digestive problems,
particularly excess stomach acid.

Creamy Fruit and Nut

Beginning the day with this recipe will give you a head start on your five a day.

1. In a mixing bowl, mix the seeds with the chopped fruit.

2. Place the yoghurt in your serving bowls. Add the fruit and seed mixture.

3. Drizzle with a small amount of Sweet Freedom if you want a sweeter taste. (As you start to cut out more refined carbohydrates from your diet, especially sugar, you will find your need for sweet food lessens.)

Did you know?
Linseeds are a great source of omega 3.

Ingredients:

2 tbsp seed mix (should contain linseed, sunflower, pumpkin, sesame and hemp seeds)

1 eating apple, chopped

Handful of green grapes, chopped

1 ripe pear, chopped

8 tbsp 0% fat natural Greek yoghurt

Drizzle of Sweet Freedom Dark (optional)

Nutritional information:

Vegetarian, wheat free, low sugar

Soft-boiled Egg

Nutritional information:

Vegetarian

Eggs are a rich source of selenium, iron and B vitamins

I had second thoughts about including this as most of us know how to boil an egg, but I recently watched the genius cook Heston on Channel 4 as he looked into the science of cooking a perfect boiled egg. I was so impressed with the results. If you didn't catch the programme (why not?!), I will share it with you.

1. Place the eggs in *cold* water and bring up to the boil.

2. As soon as the water starts to boil, remove from the heat, leaving the egg in the saucepan with the lid on. Set the timer for 6 minutes. You then have a perfectly cooked egg – weirdly, it works brilliantly.

3. Serve with wholegrain bread soldiers or toasted wholemeal pitta.

Tofu Scrambled Eggs

This is a great alternative to traditional scrambled eggs, and it's perfect for vegans. Tofu is a good protein source, but it also contains good levels of manganese and iron. Serve on wholemeal toast, with Garlic and Thyme Grilled Tomatoes (page 34) or with lean grilled bacon (if you are not vegan!).

1. In a bowl, mash the tofu. This is easier with a fork.

2. Then place the mashed tofu in a non-stick sauté pan and stir over a medium heat. As the tofu gets hot it should become more pliable. Add the milk until you have the consistency you like (add more milk if you like a runnier mix).

3. Add the nutritional yeast flakes and season with black pepper. Once heated and it has reached the desired consistency, you can serve.

> *TOP TIP!*
> Add some chopped vegetables for extra flavour and goodness

Did you know?
Tofu is made from soya beans, which are rich in phylonutrients and help to lower cholesterol.

Ingredients:
1 400g pack tofu (Cauldron tofu or blocks from health food stores are best)
50–100ml skimmed milk (or soya milk)
2–3 tbsp nutritional yeast flakes
Black pepper

Nutritional information:
Vegetarian, vegan, high energy, good protein source, good for your heart

Garlic and Thyme Grilled Tomatoes

Ingredients:

6 tomatoes, halved

2–3 cloves garlic, roughly
   chopped

Few sprigs thyme

Black pepper

Spray of olive oil

Nutritional information:

Vegetarian, vegan, wheat
free, gluten free

I love these tomatoes – perfect for a delicious breakfast or brunch, or as a side dish for a savoury meal.

1. Place the halved tomatoes, cut-side up, on a greased or non-stick baking tray.

2. Place the garlic and thyme on top of each tomato. Season with black pepper. Finish with a fine spray of olive oil.

3. Place under a preheated grill until they start to soften.

4. Serve immediately.

Did you know?
Tomatoes are rich in lycopene, a powerful antioxidant which has also been shown to help reduce some cancers.

Banana Toastie

So simple, yet delicious, especially when you have a craving for something sweet. Children love this, making it a great after-school snack or breakfast. I love to serve blueberries with this dish.

1. Toast your bread. Meanwhile, mash the banana with the syrup and cinnamon to taste.

2. Spread over your toast and top with a sprinkle of fresh berries.

3. Serve immediately.

Ingredients:
1–2 slices rye or
    wholemeal bread, or
    gluten-free bread
1 large banana, mashed
1 tsp Sweet Freedom Dark
    (optional)
Sprinkle of cinnamon
Handful of fresh berries

Nutritional information:
Vegetarian, vegan, gluten-free, bananas are rich in potassium, vitamin B6 and vitamin C

Ingredients:

1 apple, grated

1–2 tsp seed mixture

Nutritional information:

Vegetarian, vegan, wheat free

Apple Munchies

I learnt this trick a few years ago: grating an apple and adding some seeds really does fill you up and satisfy a craving far more than just eating an apple – try it! Here I have added a few teaspoons of seed mix, but feel free to add whatever you wish – a sweeter, naughtier version could be seeds, oats, grapes and maybe a tiny amount of dark chocolate chips.

Simply combine the two and enjoy. Perfect as a quick snack but it can also be used as a sweet topping for porridge or on top of rice pudding or fat-free natural yoghurt as a dessert.

Did you know?
Seed mix containing seeds such as flax, sunflower and pumpkin helps provide you with vitamins E and B, folic acid, manganese, magnesium and Omega 3 and 6. The vitamin C from the apple helps you utilise the vitamin E effectively.

Breakfast Juices

Smoothies and juices are a great way of getting your minimum five a day, but they are also a great stop-gap when you are feeling peckish, have a sugar craving or just need a pick-me-up. The recipes below can be used at any time of the day but I would recommend at breakfast time or for the mid-morning slump.

I have a masticating juicer called a Green Life Juicer, which is one of the best juicers I have ever used. It chews the fruit and vegetables and leaves very little waste. Unlike cheap centrifugal juicers, masticating juicers don't suck air into the juice or spin the fruit around bruising it and destroying nutrients. They are much more expensive then a centrifugal juicer (costing approximately £300), but if you are serious about juicing, it is a good long-term investment. I have had mine for 11 years, use it on a daily basis and to date I have had no faults or problems with the machine.

I don't have a special machine to make smoothies. I use my electric hand blender or my liquidiser.

> *TOP TIP!*
> If you have any smoothie or juice left, freeze into lollipop moulds – perfect for kids!

> Did you know?
> Beetroot juice can help lower blood pressure and is an excellent blood purifier. Drink one glass a day. If you don't like the taste, why not mix it with apple juice.

Serves
1–2

Ingredients:

Juice of 2 oranges

½ mango

1 banana

50g blueberries

2–3 tbsp 0% fat natural
    yoghurt

1 dsp flax oil

Nutritional information:

Vegetarian, wheat free,
gluten free, rich in omega-3

Smooth Operator

Smooth Operator is so sweet, smooth and creamy, you'd think
you are drinking something wicked rather than a nutrient-packed
smoothie. Find yourself somewhere comfortable, sit back and
enjoy!

Add all ingredients to your blender and whiz until smooth.

Serves
1–2

Ingredients:

50g blueberries

50g raspberries

2 tbsp 0% fat natural
    yoghurt

1 tbsp oats

2 tsp golden linseeds

Juice of 2–3 oranges

Nutritional information:

Vegetarian, wheat free,
high omega-3

Blue Moon

This is a lovely creamy smoothie, packed with goodness. It is a
great smoothie to start the day.

Place all the ingredients in your blender or jug if you are using an
electric stick blender. Whizz until smooth and serve immediately.

Frank Flu Zapper

This is a wonderful juice for those winter months or for when you are feeling a bit under-par. It really does pack quite a punch, with the ginger adding warmth and zing.

1. Juice the carrots, apples and ginger in your juicing machine. I squeeze the orange in my citrus press and then blend the two juices together, or you can use freshly squeezed orange juice.

2. Stir well and serve.

TOP TIP!
If you are feeling unwell, why not add half a teaspoon of vitamin C powder.

Ingredients:

1–2 carrots, roughly chopped
1–2 green apples, roughly chopped
Fresh ginger to taste (not too much!)
Juice of 2 oranges

Nutritional information:

Vegetarian, vegan, wheat free, gluten free, high in antioxidants

Chapter 5
Soups

You cannot beat the taste, simplicity and nutritional value of soups. They deserve a whole chapter to themselves!

Most soups can be frozen. You can buy special bags for freezing liquids, but I cheat and use a freezer bag which I place inside a plastic bowl or container. Fill it with your soup and freeze. Once frozen, you can remove the bowl and tie the bag. Don't forget to label and date the bags!

Enjoy these soups with wholegrain bread, toasted wholemeal pitta or rye breads with some homemade hummus (see Chapter 7).

Pear and Celeriac Soup

Celeriac is a good source of fibre and is packed with potassium, phosphorus, vitamins C and B6.

1. In a saucepan over a medium/high heat, add a spray of olive oil followed by the onion and ginger. Allow to soften for a few minutes before adding the pears and celeriac.

2. Sweat for at least 5 minutes before adding the stock.

3. Season with black pepper and add the chopped parsley.

4. Cook for 30 minutes on a low heat, allowing it to cook gently rather than at a fierce boil.

5. Using your stick blender (or liquidiser) whizz until smooth. Stir in the crème fraîche and add the chopped chives. Serve immediately.

Ingredients:

Olive oil spray

1 onion, chopped

2cm knuckle ginger, chopped

4 pears, peeled and diced

1 small celeriac, peeled and diced

400ml low-salt vegetable stock or water (or gluten-free stock)

Black pepper

Small handful of parsley, freshly chopped (or 1 tsp dried)

2 tbsp low-fat crème fraîche or 0% fat natural Greek yoghurt

Few sprigs fresh chives, chopped

Nutritional information:

Vegetarian, gluten-free

Chicken, Cumin and Harissa Soup

Ingredients:

Olive oil spray

1 red onion, finely chopped

2–3 cloves garlic, finely chopped

½ red pepper, finely chopped

1 tsp ground cumin

1–3 tsp harissa paste (depending on taste)

1 tsp paprika

1 tin chickpeas

1 tin chopped tomatoes

300g chicken, cooked

400ml low-salt chicken stock (or gluten-free)

Small handful of coriander, freshly chopped

2 tbsp 0% fat Greek natural yoghurt or low-fat crème fraîche

Nutritional information:

Gluten-free

Harissa paste can be fiery so go easy to begin with, but the combination of that with cumin gives this recipe an earthy, warming flavour.

1. Spray a little olive oil in a saucepan and over a medium/high heat cook the onion, garlic and red pepper until soft. Add the cumin, harissa paste and paprika and cook for 5 more minutes.

2. Add the remaining ingredients (except for the yoghurt or crème fraîche), including half the chopped coriander, and cook on a low/medium heat for 30 minutes.

3. Stir in the yoghurt or low-fat crème fraîche and, if desired, garnish with the remaining coriander just before serving.

Squash Soup with Spiced Yoghurt

Serves
4–6

I love this soup and the spiced yoghurt really adds to the flavour. It's a perfect autumn soup, making use of the cheap squash on offer.

1. Place a large saucepan over a medium/high heat and lightly spray it with olive oil. Sauté the onion, garlic and coriander seeds for 3–4 minutes to help soften.

2. Add the butternut squash, ground coriander and curry powder and cook for a further 3–4 minutes.

3. Add the apple before adding the stock. Put a lid on and cook on a low/medium heat for 30 minutes until the squash is tender.

4. Season to taste before liquidising. (I use my electric hand blender rather than transferring to a liquidiser – this saves washing up!)
In a separate bowl, mix the yoghurt, chilli and paprika together.

5. To serve, place the soup in your serving bowls and place a dollop of yoghurt in the centre of the soup.

Ingredients:

Olive oil spray
1 red onion, diced
1–2 cloves garlic, crushed
1 tsp coriander seeds
1 butternut squash, diced
1 tsp ground coriander
1–2 tbsp mild/medium
   curry powder
   (depending on taste)
1 cooking apple, diced
400–500ml water or low-
   salt vegetable stock (or
   gluten-free stock)
Seasoning to taste
200g 0% fat natural Greek
   yoghurt
1 chilli, finely chopped
1 tsp hot paprika

Nutritional information:

Vegetarian, gluten-free, good for your heart, rich in carotenes, vitamin C, B vitamins and fibre

Root Vegetable and Bean Soup

Serves
4–6

Ingredients:

Olive oil spray

1 red onion, chopped

2 cloves garlic, crushed

1 pepper, diced

2 sweet potatoes, diced

1 leek, finely chopped

2 carrots, diced

1 parsnip, diced

2 potatoes, diced

2 sticks celery, chopped

600ml low-salt vegetable
stock or water (or
gluten-free stock)

1 bay leaf

1 small handful of parsley,
chopped

1 tin haricot beans,
drained

50g red lentils

Black pepper

Nutritional information:

Vegetarian, vegan, gluten-free, high energy, high protein

This is a really lovely soup, perfect for filling you up on a winter's day. Make sure you dice the vegetables to an even size.

1. Place your stock pot on your hob over a medium/high heat and spray with a little olive oil. Add the onion, garlic and pepper and cook until they start to soften.

2. Add the remaining vegetables and allow to sweat for 5 minutes. Then add the remaining ingredients. Season with a little black pepper – you will not need salt if you have used stock.

3. Bring up to a low simmer and cook slowly for 30–35 minutes.

Note: If you want to use a slow cooker, simply add all the ingredients, cover with water or stock and cook for 4–6 hours.

Did you know?
A diet rich in allium vegetables (garlic, red onions, leeks) can help protect your joints from deterioration.

Rich Vegetable and Lentil Soup

Red lentils are high in fibre and help to lower cholesterol, provide vitamins, minerals and protein. All for virtually no fat and hardly any calories, sounds perfect!

1. Place a large saucepan or hob-proof casserole dish on the hob over a medium/high heat and spray very lightly with olive oil.

2. Add the onion and garlic and cook for 3–5 minutes until they start to soften.

3. Add the carrots, sweet potato, potato and parsnip and allow to sweat for 5 minutes. Then add the remaining ingredients.

4. Bring to a slow simmer and cook gently for 30–40 minutes until the vegetables are cooked.

5. Garnish with parsley and serve.

Note: You could liquidise this soup if you prefer – you may need to add more stock depending on how thick you like your soup.

TOP TIP!

This soup is packed with nutrients and antioxidants, so cooking it slowly on a low heat will help to retain them.

Ingredients:

Olive oil spray

1 onion, chopped

2 cloves garlic, roughly chopped

2 small carrots, diced

1 sweet potato, diced

1 large potato, diced

1 parsnip, diced

1 small stick celery with leaves, chopped

3 medium tomatoes, chopped

1 small apple, chopped

75g red lentils

600ml low-salt vegetable stock or water (or gluten-free stock)

100ml apple juice

1 tsp dill

1 handful of parsley, freshly chopped

2 tsp paprika

Dash of cayenne pepper

Extra parsley to serve

Nutritional information:

Vegetarian, vegan, gluten-free, good for your heart, low fat, high fibre

Smoked Cream of Split Pea Soup

Ingredients:

175g yellow split peas (or
    use green split peas or
    red lentils)
Dash of chilli oil
1 large or 2 small onions,
    finely chopped
3 cloves garlic, crushed
1 sweet potato, diced
2–3 sticks celery, finely
    sliced
2–3 tsp smoked paprika
600ml low-salt vegetable
    stock (or gluten-free)
Black pepper to taste

Nutritional information:

Vegetarian, vegan, gluten-
free, high in fibre, helps
lower cholesterol, good for
your heart

Traditionally this kind of soup would contain ham or bacon, but I have avoided this in order to make the soup lower in fat. Instead I have added chilli oil and smoked paprika for an extra kick – yummy.

1. Steep the split peas in hot water for an hour and then drain.

2. Place a saucepan on your hob over a medium/high heat and add a dash of chilli oil. Add the onion and garlic and cook until they start to soften.

3. Add the remaining ingredients, including the split peas.

4. Cook on a low heat for 30–40 minutes, adding more stock if needed.

5. Liquidise, adding more liquid if you prefer a thinner soup. To serve, add some extra smoked paprika and a drizzle of chilli oil.

Did you know?

Split peas are high in fibre, so excellent for keeping your digestion strong and healthy. They also stabilise blood sugar and help reduce cholesterol.

Carrot and Coriander Soup

1. Place your saucepan or casserole dish on the hob over a medium/high heat and spray with olive oil. Add the onion and garlic and cook for 5 minutes so that they start to soften.

2. Add the carrot and celery and sweat for 5 minutes, before adding the coriander and cumin.

3. Add the stock and bring to a slow simmer. Cook gently for 30 minutes.

4. Liquidise the soup, adding more liquid if necessary. Season to taste and reheat gently. Serve garnished with a few chopped coriander leaves.

Ingredients:

Olive oil spray
1 large onion, finely
    chopped
1 clove garlic, crushed
400g carrot, diced
1 stick celery, diced
2 tsp ground coriander
1 tsp ground cumin
750ml low-salt vegetable
    stock or water (or
    gluten-free stock)
Black pepper
Sprinkle of coriander
    leaves, finely chopped

Nutritional information:

Vegetarian, vegan, gluten-free

Ingredients:

1 red onion, finely
chopped

1 clove garlic, crushed

1 stick celery, finely
chopped

1 carrot, finely chopped or
grated

1kg tomatoes, chopped (if
you prefer a smooth
soup you can remove
the skins but I never
bother) (or 2–3 tins)

50g red lentils

200g vegetable stock (or
gluten-free)

Handful of fresh basil
leaves

Black pepper

Sea salt

Nutritional information:

Vegetarian, gluten-free

Healthy Tomato and Basil

A family favourite, with a few tweaks to add extra nutrients.

1. Place all the ingredients in a large stock pot and bring up to a low simmer.

2. Cook gently for 30 minutes.

3. Liquidise and then return the soup to the pan to reheat.

4. Season to taste and serve.

Leek and Potato Soup

A family favourite – I hope you enjoy it!

1. Spray your pan with olive oil and place on the hob over a medium/high heat. Cook the leeks for 5 minutes until they start to soften. Add the potato and sweat for a further 5 minutes.

2. Cover with the stock. Place on a low heat and cook slowly for 30 minutes.

3. Add the milk, crème fraîche, black pepper, parsley and sage and cook for a further 5 minutes.

4. Allow to cool slightly. Use an electric hand blender to purée and return the soup to the pan until you are ready to serve.

5. Garnish with chopped chives.

Ingredients:

Olive oil spray

2–3 leeks, sliced or chopped

2 potatoes, cubed

450ml low-salt vegetable stock (or gluten-free stock)

200ml skimmed milk

4 tbsp low-fat crème fraîche

Black pepper to taste

Small handful of parsley, freshly chopped (or 1 tsp dried parsley)

1 tbsp fresh sage

½ tsp chives, chopped

Nutritional information:

Vegetarian

49

Roasted Pumpkin Soup

1 small pumpkin
Spray of olive oil
1 onion, finely chopped
2–3 cloves garlic, crushed
1 tsp root ginger, grated
1 tsp fresh nutmeg, grated
½ tsp ground coriander
1–2 carrots, chopped
1 sweet potato, diced
2 sticks celery, chopped
4 tomatoes, peeled and
    chopped
2 tsp tomato purée
    (optional)
500ml water or low-salt
    vegetable stock (or
    gluten-free stock)
15ml lemon juice
Seasoning to taste
Drizzle of chilli oil to serve
    (optional)

Nutritional information:

Vegetarian, vegan, gluten-
free, high in fibre

The humble pumpkin is low in calories but packed with nutrients, including beta carotene. This recipe makes a delicious treat for Halloween, or you can use other squash for an all-year-round soup.

1. Cut the pumpkin into wedges, leaving the skin on. Coat with a light spray of olive oil and place in the oven on a low heat (160°C/Gas Mark 3) for 20 minutes. Meanwhile, prepare the vegetables.

2. Cook the onion, garlic and spices together in a saucepan on your hob over a medium/high heat until the onion is soft and translucent.

3. Take the flesh from the pumpkin wedges and place with the spices. Add all other ingredients. Turn to low and cook slowly for 30 minutes.

4. Allow to cool slightly. Then use an electric hand blender to purée and return the soup to the pan until you are ready to serve.

5. To serve, season as required and, for extra flavour, drizzle with chilli oil. For impressive presentation, use hollowed-out pumpkins as serving dishes!

Red Pepper and Tomato Soup with Pesto Swirl

Ingredients:

Olive oil spray

1 large onion, chopped

1–2 cloves garlic crushed

4 red peppers, seeded and
chopped

½ tsp chilli powder

8–10 fresh tomatoes,
peeled and chopped

1 tsp paprika

500ml water or low-salt
vegetable stock (or
gluten-free stock)

Black pepper to taste

Pesto (fresh or jar)

Nutritional information:

Vegetarian

1. Spray a little olive oil into the base of your saucepan. Add the onion, garlic and peppers and cook over a medium/high heat until soft and the onions are translucent. Add the chilli powder and stir well.

2. Add the tomatoes and cook for 2 minutes. Add the paprika and water or stock and cook slowly over a low heat for 30 minutes.

3. Allow to cool slightly and then use an electric hand blender to purée.

4. Reheat the soup when you are ready to serve. Place in bowls and add a spoon of pesto (see Chapter 7 for recipes to make your own) to the centre of each one. Using a sharp knife, swirl the pesto from the centre of the bowl.

Did you know?

If you are picking your own homegrown tomatoes, pick some stalks to add to the tomatoes when cooking or roasting. This increases the tomato flavour. Just remove the stalks before serving.

Mint and Green Pea Soup

This is a lovely recipe when peas are in season. It also works with frozen peas, but it does create a different flavour.

1. Spray a little oil in a pan and place on your hob over a medium/high heat. Add the spring onions and cook for 2 minutes. Add the pea pods and cook for a further 2 minutes.

2. Add the stock or water, peas and mint and season with black pepper. Cook gently on a low heat for 45 minutes to 1 hour.

3. Cool slightly. Use an electric hand blender to purée and then return the soup to the pan until you are ready to serve. Alternatively, place in the fridge to serve chilled.

4. To serve, add a dollop of low-fat crème fraîche to the centre of each bowl and swirl from the centre. Garnish with a sprig of fresh mint.

Ingredients:

Olive oil spray
4–6 spring onions, chopped to include most of the green stalks
Small handful of fresh pea pods, finely chopped (ignore this if you are using frozen peas)
500ml low-salt vegetable stock or water (or gluten-free stock)
400g fresh peas (or frozen if out of season)
2–3 sprigs fresh mint
Black pepper to season
Low-fat crème fraîche and sprig of fresh mint to garnish

Nutritional information:

Vegetarian, gluten-free, high in fibre, packed with antioxidants

Avocado Soup

Avocados contain oleic acid which has been shown to help reduce cholesterol. Use up your over ripe avocados for this soup. You can serve it hot or cold.

1. Place the avocados, lemon, garlic and chilli in a liquidiser and blend until smooth.

2. Add the hot stock and crème fraîche and whizz again. Season to taste.

3. Serve hot or cold, garnished with chopped avocado.

Ingredients:

3 ripe avocados

Juice and zest of 1 lemon

1–2 cloves garlic, crushed

1 chilli, finely chopped

750ml low-salt chicken or vegetable stock, heated (or gluten-free)

200g low-fat crème fraîche

Seasoning to taste

Extra avocado to serve, chopped

Nutritional information:

Vegetarian, high in fibre, rich in potassium, gluten-free

Tomato and Chilli Soup

Ingredients:

Olive oil spray

1 red onion, finely
  chopped

2 cloves garlic, crushed

1–2 chillies (depending on
  personal preference),
  finely chopped

500g fresh tomatoes,
  peeled and finely
  chopped

2 tsp sundried tomato
  purée

50g sundried tomatoes

½ stick celery, finely
  chopped

450ml water

1 heaped tsp paprika

Black pepper to taste

Drizzle of chilli oil to serve

Nutritional information:

Vegetarian, vegan, gluten-
free, high in lycopene

Tomato soup never fails to cheer me up – it is like a hug in a bowl or mug. This recipe contains chillies, which not only taste delicious but also help speed up your metabolism. If you don't fancy the heat, just omit the chillies.

1. Spray a little olive oil in a pan and place on your hob over a medium/high heat. Add the onion and garlic. Cook until translucent.

2. Add all of the remaining ingredients to the pan and leave to cook slowly on a low heat for 30 minutes.

3. Cool slightly. Liquidise to a purée, adding more liquid if required.

4. Serve with a drizzle of chilli oil for an extra kick.

Did you know?
Chillies have an anti-inflammatory effect.

Minestrone Soup

1. Heat a spray of olive oil in the base of your casserole dish or heavy saucepan over a medium/high heat. Add the onion and garlic and cook until translucent and soft. Add the pepper and cook for another 2 minutes.

2. Place all of the remaining ingredients, except for the cabbage, spaghetti and basil, into the pan and cook slowly on a low heat for 30–40 minutes.

3. Fifteen minutes before serving, add the shredded cabbage, dried spaghetti (broken into smaller pieces) and basil.

4. Serve with crusty wholemeal bread and hummus for a hearty meal.

Ingredients:

Olive oil spray
1 large red onion, chopped
1 clove garlic, crushed
1 carrot, diced
1 red pepper, finely
   chopped
½ stick celery, finely
   chopped
3–4 fresh tomatoes,
   peeled and chopped
1 tin red kidney beans
50g fresh green beans,
   chopped
600ml water or low-salt
   vegetable stock (or
   gluten-free stock)
3 tsp pure tomato purée
½ tsp cayenne pepper
1 tsp paprika
2 bay leaves
Seasoning to taste
75g cabbage, shredded
60g spaghetti (or gluten-
   free)
1 tbsp fresh basil,
   chopped

Nutritional information:
Vegetarian, vegan, gluten-
free, high in fibre

57

Carrot and Courgette Soup

Ingredients:

Olive oil spray

1 red onion, chopped

2–3 carrots, diced

1 sweet potato, diced

1–2 tsp fresh ginger, grated

600ml low-salt vegetable stock (or gluten-free)

1 tsp dried or fresh thyme

2–3 courgettes, diced

Nutritional information:

Vegetarian, vegan, gluten-free, high in fibre, aids digestion

The sweet potato and carrot make this recipe rich in beta carotene and antioxidants.

1. Place a pan on your hob over a medium/high heat and spray with olive oil. Cook the onion until soft and translucent.

2. Add the carrots and sweet potato and cook for a further couple of minutes to help soften. Add the fresh ginger and cook for another minute.

3. Add all remaining ingredients. Place on a low heat and cook slowly for 30–40 minutes.

4. You can leave the soup as is. If you prefer a smooth soup, allow it to cool slightly and then purée with an electric hand blender. Return the soup to the pan until you are ready to serve.

Tomato, Lentil and Carrot Soup

This is a family favourite – packed with nutrients.

1. Spray the base of your saucepan with olive oil and place on your hob over a medium/high heat. Cook the onion, garlic and paprika together until the onion is soft and translucent.

2. Add the remaining ingredients except for the basil.

3. Cover with water or stock. Place on a low heat and cook slowly for 30 minutes.

4. Cool slightly. Then purée with an electric hand blender and return to pan until you are ready to serve.

5. Serve garnished with chopped basil.

Ingredients:

Olive oil spray

1 large red onion, diced

1–2 cloves garlic, crushed (optional)

2 tsp paprika

6–8 tomatoes, chopped (you can use tinned chopped tomatoes but the flavour is slightly different)

2 carrots, chopped

125g lentils, washed

1 tbsp tomato purée

½ red pepper, chopped

570ml water or low-salt vegetable stock (or gluten-free stock)

1 bay leaf

1 tsp dried basil or bunch of fresh basil, chopped, to garnish

Nutritional information:

Vegetarian, vegan, gluten-free, high in fibre, rich in antioxidants, good for your heart

Chapter 6
Salads and vegetable dishes

Salads are not just for garnish! Enjoy these salads as a main meal by combining two or three, or try combining something like the Savoury Rice Salad with the Mixed Bean Salad for lunch – ideal for packed lunches and very filling.

Dressings often contain lots of hidden fat and calories. There are some alternatives offered in the following recipes but if you are stuck on your mayonnaise, opt for the lowest fat version.

Savoury Rice Salad

Brown rice is a great source of energy. It is high in magnesium and manganese, phyto-oestrogens and B vitamins. It really pays to swap your white rice for brown!

1. Place the rice in a saucepan, cover with boiling water and boil for 10 minutes without the lid. Then place the lid on the saucepan and remove from the heat. Leave to one side and the rice will continue cooking in its own heat. After 10–15 minutes, check that it is cooked by fluffing with a fork.

2. Meanwhile, steam the green beans and peas for 3–4 minutes until barely tender. Cool immediately by placing in a bowl of cold or iced water.

3. In a large salad serving dish, place the cooked rice. Add the green beans, peas, chilli, red onion, pepper, sweetcorn and mint. Mix well.

4. In a jug, mix the lemon juice and zest, cayenne, olive oil and black pepper. Stir well and use to dress the salad when you are ready to serve.

Did you know?
Basmati rice is low in glycaemic load.

Ingredients:

160g brown or Basmati rice
400ml boiling water
75g green beans, chopped
60g peas
1 chilli, finely chopped
1 large red onion, finely chopped
1 red pepper, chopped
50g sweetcorn (tinned or frozen)
Small handful of mint, freshly chopped
Juice and zest of 1 lemon
½ tsp cayenne pepper
1–2 tbsp extra virgin olive oil (or omega-rich oil)
Black pepper
Seasoning to taste

Nutritional information:

Vegetarian, vegan, gluten-free

Baby Spinach and Apple Salad

Ingredients:

1 handful of washed baby
leaf spinach per serving

½ apple, finely sliced, per
serving

Nutritional information:

Vegetarian, vegan, gluten-
free

I apologise for the simplicity of this recipe but, really, it is a delicious side salad so just had to be included!

1. Simply mix the spinach and apple together. If you prefer a dressing, use a low-fat vinaigrette.

Apple and Kiwi Salad

1. Place the washed leaves in a bowl, add the parsley and chives and combine.

2. Add the diced cucumber, celery, apples and kiwi slices.

3. In a small bowl, combine the white wine vinegar with the oil. Season to taste.

4. Dress the salad, toss well and serve immediately.

Note: If you want to make this salad in advance, toss the apple in lemon juice to prevent it from going brown.

Ingredients:

100g mixed salad leaves (such as rocket, watercress, cos lettuce, baby leaf spinach, escarole)

1 tbsp fresh parsley, finely chopped

1 tbsp chives, chopped

½ small cucumber, diced

2 sticks celery, diced

2 large apples, diced

4 kiwi fruit, peeled and sliced

1 tbsp white wine vinegar

2 tbsp extra virgin olive oil or omega-rich oil

Black pepper to taste

Nutritional information:

Vegetarian, vegan, gluten-free, rich in vitamin C

Rainbow Low-fat Coleslaw

This coleslaw is a low-fat version. You could cheat and use a very low-fat mayonnaise, but I prefer the yoghurt variety which is much healthier. I normally make a large batch and keep it in the fridge for times when I am searching for a snack. For ease, I use my food processor as it grates the cabbage and carrot in seconds.

1. Shred the cabbage and carrots in your food processor (or grate by hand). Place in a large bowl. Add the apple and grapes.

2. In a small bowl, mix the yoghurt, lemon zest and juice, wholegrain mustard and black pepper. Add a little water if you prefer a more fluid dressing.

3. Combine the dressing with the coleslaw.

4. Serve with salads, jacket potatoes or as a side dish.

Note: Why not add a large handful of mixed seeds to make a Nutty Rainbow Coleslaw (vegetarian).

New Potato Salad

1. Place the cooked potatoes, spring onions, cucumber and herbs in a large bowl. Combine well.

2. In a small bowl, mix the yoghurt, lemon zest and juice, wholegrain mustard and black pepper. Add a little water if you prefer a more fluid dressing.

3. Combine the dressing with the potato salad.

4. Serve with other salads or as a side dish.

Ingredients:

750g new potatoes, cooked

4–6 spring onions, finely chopped including the green stalks

½ cucumber, diced

1 tbsp mint, freshly chopped

1 tbsp chives, freshly chopped

1 tbsp parsley, freshly chopped

3–4 tbsp 0% fat Greek yoghurt (or very low-fat mayonnaise)

Zest and juice of ½ lemon

½ tsp wholegrain mustard

Black pepper to taste

Nutritional information:

Vegetarian, gluten-free

Wild Rice and Lentil Salad

Ingredients:

4 tomatoes, cut into
  wedges

1–2 red peppers, cut into
  wedges

Olive oil spray

Black pepper

Sea salt

175g rice mix

125g brown lentils

75g puy lentils

4–6 spring onions, finely
  chopped including the
  green stalks

Small handful of fresh
  mint, finely chopped

Nutritional information:

Vegetarian, vegan, gluten-
free

This is a really wholesome dish. Buy a wild and red rice blend, available from wholefood shops. You can add any salad leaves to this, but I prefer it quite simple. Feel free to add whatever other herbs or seasoning you wish.

1. Preheat the oven to 200°C (Gas Mark 6).

2. Place the tomatoes and peppers in a roasting dish. Spray with a little olive oil and season with black pepper and sea salt.

3. Place in the oven and bake for 15–20 minutes.

4. Meanwhile, place the rice in a pan, cover with water and cook as per the packet's instructions. I normally cover with water, bring to the boil and simmer for 5–7 minutes. Then I pop on the saucepan lid, remove from the heat completely and leave to finish cooking.

5. While the rice is cooking, add the lentils to another pan, cover with water and cook until they start to soften. This should take about 10 minutes – they should still have bite and not be soggy. Drain and leave to one side.

6. Mix the rice and lentils together. Add the roasted, chopped tomatoes and peppers, and the spring onion. Stir in the mint leaves.

7. Serve warm or cold.

TOP TIP!
If you like a dressing on your salad, use a low fat vinaigrette.

Ingredients:

800g cooked or tinned
    mixed beans (e.g.
    kidney, chickpea,
    butterbean, flageolet)
250g edamame (soya)
    beans (fresh or frozen)
1 tbsp basil, chopped
1 tbsp parsley, chopped
Seasoning
2–3 tbsp low-fat
    vinaigrette dressing
75g French beans

Nutritional information:

Vegetarian, vegan, gluten-
free, aids digestion, high
in fibre

Mixed Bean Salad

A delicious salad that is packed with nutrients and very satisfying as it is high in protein and so will keep you feeling fuller for longer.

1. Cook the edamame (soya) beans if you are using frozen. Follow the packet's instructions or boil in water for 3–4 minutes and then drain.

2. Place the edamame and mixed beans in a serving dish.

3. Add the chopped herbs and season to taste.

4. Add the vinaigrette dressing and combine gently.

5. Boil or steam the French beans for 3–4 minutes. Then drain and add to the salad. Serve.

Red Cabbage, Apple and Orange Salad

Serves

4

A zesty coleslaw!

1. Place the shredded cabbage in a large salad-serving bowl. Add the finely sliced spring onions.

2. Grate the zest of 1 orange into a jug. Peel and segment the 3 oranges and add to the cabbage and onion. Add the apple before combining well.

3. Add the lemon zest and juice to the orange zest. Add the wholegrain mustard and stir well. Season with black pepper.

4. Pour over the cabbage mixture and combine well before serving.

Ingredients:

250g red cabbage, finely
   shredded
3 spring onions, finely
   sliced
3 oranges
2 dessert apples, diced
Zest and juice of ½ lemon
1 tsp wholegrain mustard
Black pepper

Nutritional information:

Vegetarian, vegan, gluten-
free

Warm Beetroot Salad

2–3 beetroots, peeled and
   cubed

2–3 parsnips, peeled and
   cubed

1–2 small sweet potatoes,
   peeled and cubed

Olive oil spray

1 tsp dried oregano

Sea salt

Black pepper

Balsamic vinegar

4 generous handfuls of
   seasonal salad leaves,
   washed

1 red onion, chopped (or
   spring onions, sliced)

1 red pepper, sliced

100g reduced fat feta,
   crumbled

Nutritional information:

Vegetarian, gluten-free

Beetroot is a great blood purifier. It is rich in bioflavonoids, carotenoids, vitamin C, folic acid and manganese. This recipe is truly delicious.

1. Preheat the oven to 200°C (Gas Mark 6).

2. Place the root vegetables (all cubed to a similar size) in a roasting tin.

3. Spray with olive oil, ensuring it is all evenly coated. Sprinkle with oregano, sea salt, black pepper and a drizzle of balsamic.

4. Place in the oven and cook for 20 minutes, or until soft and sweet.

5. Meanwhile, place the leaf salad in your serving dishes. Add the red onion (or spring onions) and the red pepper. Toss to ensure everything is evenly distributed.

6. When the vegetables are cooked, simply place them in the centre of your leaf salad and finish with a sprinkle of feta cheese. Serve immediately.

Spicy Roasted Sweet Potato with Yoghurt Dressing

1. Preheat your oven to 200°C (Gas Mark 6).

2. In an ovenproof dish, add the swect potatoes, onion and garlic, and spray with olive oil. Place in your oven and cook for 15 minutes.

3. Meanwhile, finely chop the chilli, grate the ginger and crush the coriander and cumin. Mix together thoroughly with the turmeric. Season to taste.

4. Remove the potatoes from the oven and sprinkle the spices over. Carefully toss again, ensuring it is all covered well. If necessary, you can add a little spray of oil but it should only be lightly covered.

5. Place back in the oven for another 10–15 minutes until the potatoes are soft.

6. Once soft, remove and place in a serving dish. Add the chopped coriander leaves and serve with a dollop of yoghurt.

Ingredients:

- 3 sweet potatoes, evenly diced
- 2 red onions, quartered
- 2–4 cloves garlic, roughly chopped
- Olive oil spray
- 1 chilli
- 2.5–5cm knuckle of fresh ginger
- 2 tsp coriander seeds
- 2 tsp cumin seeds
- 1 tsp turmeric
- Seasoning
- Handful of fresh coriander leaves, chopped
- 2–3 tbsp 0% fat Greek yoghurt

Nutritional information:

Vegetarian, gluten-free

Rainbow Bean and Feta Salad

1 red onion, sliced

1–2 peppers, various
colours, sliced

½ cucumber, thickly diced

1 large carrot, grated

1 apple, diced

8–12 cherry tomatoes,
halved

8–10 sugar snap peas,
chopped

1 tin borlotti beans,
drained

1 tin chickpeas, drained

1 handful of flat leaf
parsley, chopped

1 chilli (optional, but great
if you like an extra kick)

2 tbsp olive oil (or flax oil)

Juice of ½ lemon

1–2 tsp balsamic vinegar

Black pepper

Sea salt or low-sodium salt
(optional)

120g low-fat feta

Nutritional information:

Vegetarian, gluten-free,
high in fibre, good for
your heart, aids digestion

I love this salad – not only does it look ultra healthy and vibrant,
it also tastes delicious. Feta is a good source of calcium, B12 and
B2, but it is high in fat so opt for a low fat version.

1. Place all the ingredients apart from the oil, lemon, balsamic
vinegar, seasoning and feta in a large bowl. Combine well.

2. Mix the olive oil, lemon juice and balsamic vinegar together.
Taste and adjust to suit your palate. Season to taste.

3. Just before serving, add the dressing, toss well and crumbled
the feta over the top of the salad.

Note: This is also lovely when stuffed in wholemeal pitta.

Asian-style Pasta Salad

I love this combination. It's a meal in itself or you can serve it as a tasty side dish – perfect with some Asian-inspired baked salmon. If you are using this as a side dish, you may want to halve the recipe (but not the dressing!).

1. Cook the pasta following the packet's instructions. Drain and rinse with cold water, before placing in your salad bowl.

2. Mix the sesame oil, soy, ginger, chilli and lime zest and juice together. Leave to one side to infuse.

3. Add the soya beans, mange tout, sugar snap peas, grated carrot, spring onions, alfalfa sprouts, pumpkin seeds and coriander to the pasta. Combine well.

4. When you are ready to serve, pour on the dressing and toss to combine the flavours.

5. Cut the pomegranate in half, squeeze the juice over and allow the seeds to fall into the pasta salad, making sure none of the pith falls in.

6. Serve immediately.

Ingredients:

300g wholemeal pasta (or gluten-free)

1 tsp sesame oil

1 tbsp soy sauce

2cm knuckle ginger, finely chopped or grated

1 chilli, finely chopped

Zest and juice of 1 lime

200g soya beans

100g mange tout

100g sugar snap peas, cut into thirds

2 carrots, grated

4–5 spring onions, finely chopped

50g alfalfa sprouts

30g pumpkin seeds

Small handful of coriander, roughly chopped

1 pomegranate

Nutritional information:

Vegetarian, vegan, gluten-free

Colourful Herb and Feta Salad

Ingredients:

1 red onion, finely sliced

1 pepper (or 2 halves of
differently coloured
peppers)

¼ cucumber, chopped

12 cherry tomatoes,
halved

1 apple, diced

1 orange, diced

1 tin chickpeas, drained

Handful of baby leaf
spinach

Handful of rocket

Handful of watercress

Small handful of flat leaf
parsley

2 tbsp mint, roughly
chopped

2 tbsp extra virgin olive oil
or flax oil

Juice and zest of ½ lemon

1 tbsp balsamic vinegar

Black pepper

125g low-fat feta,
crumbled

Nutritional information:

Vegetarian, gluten-free,
high in fibre

This is such a versatile recipe. Simply use whatever colourful
vegetables, fruit and herbs you have. Sprinkle with low-fat feta
and drizzle with your dressing – delicious!

1. Place all of the salad ingredients and herbs in a salad bowl and
combine well.

2. In a jug, mix the oil, lemon and vinegar. Combine and season
with black pepper to taste.

3. Just before serving, add the crumbled feta and the dressing.
Toss well.

Puy Lentil Salad

So simple, but really delicious and packed with nutrients.

1. Place a pan sprayed with olive oil on your hob over a low heat. Cook the onion and garlic slowly until the onion begins to darken and caramelise.

2. Meanwhile, place the puy lentils in a saucepan, cover with water and simmer for 15–20 minutes. Drain and place in your salad bowl.

3. Add the cooked onion and garlic, the lemon zest and juice and the dried mint. Combine well and season to taste.

4. Serve hot or cold.

Note: This recipe also works well with a balsamic vinegar dressing.

Ingredients:

Olive oil spray
1 red onion, finely
    chopped
2–3 cloves garlic, roughly
    chopped
300g puy lentils
Zest and juice of ½ lemon
1 tsp dried mint
Seasoning

Nutritional information:

Vegetarian, vegan, gluten-free

Hot Courgette, Red Onion, Chilli and Spinach Salad

Ingredients:

Olive oil spray

3–4 courgettes, cut into
sticks

1 large red onion, sliced

1 red chilli, roughly
chopped

Black pepper

100g baby spinach

Chilli oil

Nutritional information:

Vegetarian, vegan, gluten-
free

This is perfect as a side dish for many meals but especially fish.

1. Spray your sauté pan with olive oil. Add the courgettes and red onion and cook over a medium heat until they start to soften.

2. Add the chilli and cook for another minute. Season with black pepper.

3. Finally stir in the spinach, only leaving it long enough so that it starts to wilt slightly. Remove from the pan immediately and serve with a drizzle of chilli oil.

Roasted Red Onion, Beetroot and Pepper Salad with Pine Nuts

1. Place the pine nuts on a baking tray, spread out evenly. Place under a medium grill and roast for a couple of minutes until they start to brown. Be careful as they can catch very quickly, so don't wander off! Then remove the pine nuts and keep to one side.

2. Preheat the oven to 200°C (Gas Mark 6).

3. Place the onion, beetroot and red pepper on a baking tray. Spray with olive oil, sprinkle with sea salt and black pepper and a drizzle of balsamic vinegar. Bake for 20–30 minutes.

4. Mix the extra virgin olive oil with 1 tbsp balsamic vinegar. Mix well and season to taste.

5. Remove the roasted vegetables from the oven. Place the salad leaves on your serving plates. Add the roasted vegetables, combining well.

6. Sprinkle with pine nuts and finish with a drizzle of the dressing.

7. Serve immediately.

Ingredients:

3 red onions, cut into
   wedges
2 beetroots, cut into
   wedges
2 red peppers, cut into
   wedges
Olive oil spray
Sea salt
Black pepper
Balsamic vinegar
75g pine nuts
2 tbsp extra virgin olive oil
Mixed salad leaves

Nutritional information:

Vegetarian, vegan, gluten-
free

Chapter 7
On the side...

Here is a selection of recipes for side dishes, condiments and dips, all made with a healthy twist. We all love roast potatoes, wedges and chips but follow the recipes below as they are much healthier. Many diet cookbooks recommend jacket potatoes as a healthy option but actually they are high GI (meaning they give your blood sugar a sudden surge!), so use them wisely. It is far better to have new potatoes or sweet potato, brown rice, basmati or wholegrain pasta to accompany your main meal.

Potato Wedges

Serves
2–4

1. Preheat your oven to 200°C (Gas Mark 6).

2. Place the potato wedges in a bowl with a few sprays of olive oil and the paprika. Stir to ensure the potatoes are all evenly covered with the oil and paprika mixture.

3. Spray your baking tray with olive oil before transferring the potatoes onto it.

4. Place in the oven and cook for 25–30 minutes until golden, turning occasionally.

Variations: Add chopped garlic, chillies and herbs of your choice for extra spice.

Ingredients:
3–4 large potatoes, cut into wedges but with skins left on
Olive oil spray
1–2 tsp paprika

Nutritional information:
Vegetarian, vegan, gluten-free

Baked New Potatoes

Serves
4–5

This must be the simplest recipe of all!

1. Preheat the oven to 210°C (Gas Mark 6).

2. Place the potatoes in a bowl. Spray lightly with olive oil before adding the garlic, paprika and herbs. Stir well, ensuring all of the potatoes are coated. This will create a vibrant red/gold colour.

3. Spray your baking tray with olive oil. Pour on the potatoes and place in the oven.

4. Bake for approximately 35–45 minutes, until golden.

Ingredients:
1kg new potatoes, washed
Olive oil spray
2–3 cloves garlic, crushed
2–3 tsp mixed herbs (fresh or dried)
2–3 tsp paprika
Seasoning to taste

Nutritional information:
Vegetarian, vegan, gluten-free

Guilt-free Roast Potatoes

Ingredients:

3–4 large potatoes, peeled
    and cut in half or thirds
Paprika
1–2 tbsp semolina
Few sprigs of rosemary
    (optional)

Nutritional information:

Vegetarian, vegan, gluten-
free

This recipe may at first seem a bit odd and unappetising but believe me, it really is okay as long as you don't skimp on the paprika!

1. Place the potatoes in a steamer or boil for 7–8 minutes until they are just starting to go soft on the outer edges.

2. Drain and place back in the empty saucepan.

3. Add 1–2 tbsp paprika and the semolina. Shake to bash the potatoes slightly and cover in the paprika.

4. Place about 2–3cm of boiling water in the bottom of your roasting tin. Carefully add the potatoes so that they don't splash or move around too much.

5. Place in the oven and cook for 30–45 minutes. By this time the water will have evaporated and the tops of the potatoes should start to crisp. Turn them, so the bottoms can now crisp. Add more paprika as you go and, if you are using it, you can now add the rosemary.

6. Cook until the potatoes reach your desired crispiness.

Note: Using semolina and paprika on your normal oil-cooked roast potatoes will create a really crispy roast with a delicious flavour. Remember the secret when using oil is to get it as hot as possible before adding the potatoes, then turn them halfway through cooking and add more paprika.

Serves
3–4

Homemade Golden Chips

Ingredients:

4–5 large potatoes, sliced
    into chips
Olive oil spray
Paprika (optional)
Sea salt

Nutritional information:

Vegetarian, vegan, gluten-
free

Who can resist chips? These are made using spray oil. (I place olive oil in a disused spray container as this is cheaper than buying spray oils.) By using spray oils you cut down on the amount of fat in the chips, making them a guilt-free indulgence.

1. Preheat your oven to 210°C (Gas Mark 6).

2. Place the chopped potatoes in a bowl of water for a few minutes. Then drain and steam or boil for 5 minutes.

3. Meanwhile spray your baking tray with olive oil.

4. Drain the potatoes and place on the baking tray in a single layer. Spray with a little more olive oil and sprinkle with paprika (this is optional but helps to create a golden colour and nice flavour).

5. Place on the low rack and bake for 10–15 minutes before turning over, spraying again and cooking for another 10–15 minutes or until they are cooked. The cooking times depend on the thickness of your chips.

6. To serve, sprinkle with sea salt.

Homemade Sweet Potato Chips

Serves
3–4

Sweet potatoes are packed with beta carotene. They are also high in fibre and rich in potassium and vitamins C and A.

1. Preheat your oven to 210°C (Gas Mark 6).

2. Spray your baking tray with olive oil. Place the sweet potatoes on the baking tray in a single layer. Spray with a little more olive oil and sprinkle with paprika. (This helps to create a golden colour and nice flavour.)

3. Place in the oven and bake for 10–15 minutes before turning over, spraying again and adding a sprinkle of fresh or dried chilli flakes. Cook for another 10–15 minutes or until the chips are cooked. The cooking times depend on the thickness of your chips.

4. To serve, sprinkle with sea salt and more chilli flakes if preferred.

Ingredients:
3–4 large sweet potatoes, sliced into chips
Olive oil spray
Paprika
Fresh or dried chilli flakes
Sea salt

Nutritional information:
Vegetarian, vegan, gluten-free

Sundried Tomato and Basil Pesto

Ingredients:

125g sundried tomatoes

1 large handful of basil

40g pine nuts

3–4 cloves garlic, peeled

2–3 tbsp extra virgin olive
    oil

Seasoning to taste

Nutritional information:

Vegetarian, vegan, gluten-
free

If you love pesto but don't want the added cheese, this recipe is perfect. It delivers great flavour, perfect for adding to wholemeal pasta, as a topping for a healthy pizza or stuffed in a chicken breast.

1. Place all the ingredients in your food processor or blender and whizz until smooth and combined.

2. Pour into a dish, cover, and place in the fridge for at least 30 minutes, allowing the flavours to infuse.

3. Store in the fridge in an airtight container until you are ready to use. You can also freeze this pesto. I normally place it in a silicon ice-cube tray and pop out a few cubes when I need them.

Watercress and Spinach Pesto

I love this with pasta or as a topping on bruschetta. Watercress has a strong flavour so this recipe only uses 50g, but if you like the flavour you can add more (and reduce the quantity of spinach accordingly).

1. Place all the ingredients in your food processor or blender and whizz until smooth and combined.

2. Pour into a dish, cover, and place in the fridge for at least 30 minutes, allowing the flavours to infuse.

3. Store in the fridge in an airtight container until you are ready to use. You can also freeze this pesto. I normally place it in a silicon ice-cube tray and pop out a few cubes when I need them.

Ingredients:

450g baby leaf spinach

50g watercress

3 garlic cloves, peeled

2–3 tbsp olive oil

50g pine nuts

75g low-fat feta cheese

Black pepper

Nutritional information:

Vegetarian, gluten-free

Did you know?
Spinach is rich in calcium, magnesium, manganese, iron, vitamins A and K, and B vitamins. Recommended to those who suffer from osteoporosis, and the calcium, magnesium and vitamin K can help lower the risk of its development.

Salsa

Ingredients:

2 red peppers, diced

1–2 chillies, diced

½ cucumber, diced

1 red onion, diced

3 tomatoes, diced

2–3 cloves garlic, crushed

Small handful of flat leaf
    parsley, chopped

1 dsp balsamic vinegar

2 dsp extra virgin olive oil

Zest of 1 lemon

Black pepper

Nutritional information:

Vegetarian, vegan, gluten-
free

When making a salsa, try to dice the vegetables to a similar in size. Salsa can be used as dip with fresh vegetables. It's also delicious with grilled meat or fish.

1. In a bowl, add the chopped vegetables, garlic and parsley. Combine well.

2. Add the balsamic vinegar, olive oil and lemon zest. Season to taste with black pepper. Combine.

3. Leave to rest for 20 minutes for the flavours to infuse, before serving.

Hummus

Hummus is cheap, simple to make and packed with nutrients. Use it on oatcakes, wholemeal pitta, or with vegetable sticks. For an extra health boost, make it with flax oil which is great for getting some omega into your diet.

1. Place all the ingredients into a blender and whizz until smooth. Add more lemon juice or olive oil until you get the desired consistency.

2. If you taste the hummus and think it is not garlicky enough, don't be tempted to add more until you have let it rest for at least 20 minutes. Taste again before adding more.

3. Store in an airtight container in the fridge. Should last 3–4 days.

Variations:
• Pesto Hummus (vegetarian, gluten-free): add 1 tbsp pesto

• Red Pepper Hummus (vegetarian, vegan, gluten-free): add 1 sweet red pepper

• Red Pepper and Chilli Hummus (vegetarian, vegan, gluten-free): add 1 sweet red pepper, 1 chilli, finely chopped, and a dash of Tabasco sauce (optional – only if you like it very hot!)

• Lemon and Coriander Hummus (vegetarian, vegan, gluten-free): add zest and juice of 1 lemon and a handful of fresh coriander leaves

Makes
1 large pot

Ingredients:
400g chickpeas (can use tinned)
2–3 tbsp olive oil or flax oil
Juice of ½ lemon
2–4 cloves garlic (depending on personal taste), peeled
1 tbsp tahini paste

Nutritional information:
Vegetarian, vegan, gluten-free

Chapter 8
Meat

Meat can provide a meal with high protein, which is good, however be aware that it is also high in fat so opt for leaner cuts where possible. For those serious about their health, I would recommend just two or three meat meals per week. Instead opt for oily fish or vegetarian (not high dairy) meals and include lots of wholegrains, pulses and fresh vegetables. I try to buy the best quality meat I can, avoiding meats that have been processed or altered. Get to know your local butcher as they can advise on the best choices for health.

Simple Chicken Curry

You can't beat a good, homemade curry. Forget the high-fat, high-salt jars of curry sauce, this recipe uses your own homemade paste. Simply store it in the fridge in an airtight container or freeze until needed. This recipe uses chicken, but you can also use lean turkey breast or why not add some wholesome veggies? I have used low-fat coconut milk. If you can't find low fat, avoid using full-fat coconut milk as it is very calorific – instead add more yoghurt.

1. In a food processor, add the ginger, garlic, chilli, lemon grass, olive oil, small handful of coriander leaves, tomatoes and garam masala. Whizz until you form a paste. Leave to one side to rest or store in the fridge or freezer until needed.

2. In a sauté pan, heat a little olive oil over a medium heat. Add the onion and pepper and cook for a couple of minutes before adding the chicken. Continue to cook until the chicken is completely white.

3. Add half the curry paste and cook for another few minutes before adding the coconut milk and yoghurt. Taste and add more paste if you want a more potent curry.

4. Simmer on a low heat for 20 minutes until the chicken is cooked thoroughly. If the curry is too thick, add a little water.

5. Add the second handful of chopped coriander and the lime zest.

6. Stir and serve on a bed of rice, ideally brown or Basmati rice.

Ingredients:

1–3cm knuckle fresh ginger, peeled
3–4 cloves garlic, peeled
1–3 chillies (depending on strength and personal taste)
1 stick lemon grass, peeled
3 tbsp olive oil
Small handful of coriander leaves
6 tomatoes
1 tbsp garam masala
Olive oil
1 large onion, chopped
1 pepper, sliced
4 chicken breasts, diced
200ml low-fat coconut milk
3 tbsp 0% fat Greek yoghurt
Small handful of coriander leaves, chopped
Zest of 1 lime

Nutritional information:
Gluten-free

Ingredients:

1 punnet cherry tomatoes

3–4 cloves garlic, roughly
    chopped

2 sprigs thyme

Olive oil

Balsamic vinegar

Black pepper

Sea salt

Xylitol

4 chicken fillets, with all
    skin and fat removed

100g baby leaf spinach,
    washed

1 red onion, finely
    chopped

Nutritional information:

Gluten-free, good for your
heart

Griddled Chicken with Baked Tomatoes and Spinach

This is one of my favourite recipes – I love the flavours of baked tomatoes, garlic and balsamic vinegar. You can of course grill your chicken if you prefer, but I love the look of griddled chicken.

1. Preheat the oven to 200°C (Gas Mark 6).

2. Place the tomatoes in a deep baking tray and add the garlic and thyme, making sure some of it covers the tomatoes. Drizzle with olive oil and balsamic vinegar. Sprinkle with black pepper, sea salt and a little Xylitol if you like your tomatoes sweet.

3. Place in the oven and bake for 20 minutes.

4. When the tomatoes are almost ready you can start to griddle the chicken. Cook on both sides until brown and cooked thoroughly.

5. Remove the tomatoes from the oven. Place the spinach in a bowl with the chopped onion. Pour over the tomatoes and toss gently to combine.

6. Place the spinach and tomato mixture on each plate and place the chicken on top.

7. Season to taste before serving.

Did you know?

Spinach is rich in antioxidants, manganese, magnesium and beta carotene.

Tuscan-style Chicken

This dish started out as a basic one-pot tomato, garlic and basil with chicken but my son decided he wanted to bulk it out (he is a very hungry university student!) and so added beans, chopped tinned tomatoes and peppers. The result is delicious and wholesome.

1. Preheat the oven to 200°C (Gas Mark 6).

2. In a large roasting tray, add the onion, garlic, pepper, pancetta, chicken and cherry tomatoes. Make sure they are evenly distributed.

3. Drizzle with olive oil and a little balsamic vinegar.

4. Season with black pepper, sea salt and a little paprika. Add the thyme, placing it near the chicken.

5. Bake in the oven for 15 minutes.

6. Remove and add the olives, tinned tomatoes, basil leaves and beans. Add the stock or, if you are feeling daring, red wine. Combine gently.

7. Place back in the oven for another 5–10 minutes.

8. Serve immediately.

Did you know?
Beans are rich in folic acid and B vitamins.

Ingredients:

1 large red onion, cut into wedges
3–4 cloves garlic, roughly chopped
1 red pepper, thickly sliced
100g pancetta or lean bacon, thickly diced
4 chicken breasts
1 punnet cherry tomatoes
Olive oil
Balsamic vinegar
Black pepper
Sea salt
Paprika
2–3 sprigs thyme
75g olives (optional)
1 tin chopped tomatoes
Handful of basil leaves
1 tin borlotti beans, drained
1 tin haricot beans, drained
100ml chicken stock or red wine (or gluten-free stock)

Nutritional information:
Gluten-free, aids digestion

Stir-fried Beef

Ingredients:

450g lean beef steak, cut
   into thin strips
3–4 tbsp low-salt soy
   sauce
1 tbsp sesame oil
3 cloves garlic, roughly
   chopped
2–3cm knuckle ginger,
   roughly chopped
1 chilli, finely chopped
1 bunch spring onions,
   chopped
200g broccoli, cut into
   small florets
100g edamame beans
50g cashew nuts

Nutritional information:

Gluten-free

This is packed with nutrients. When using a wok, you are cooking at a high heat but for a short period of time so the nutrients are protected.

1. Place the sliced beef in a bowl and cover with the soy sauce. Leave to marinate for 20 minutes at room temperature. Meanwhile, prepare all the vegetables.

2. When you are ready to start cooking, place the sesame oil in the wok over a high heat. Add the beef and cook for 2–3 minutes. Then remove the beef and leave to one side.

3. Add the remaining ingredients except for the edamame beans and cashew nuts and stir fry for another 2–3 minutes.

4. Add the beef and cook for 1–2 more minutes. Then add the edamame beans and cashew nuts and serve on a bed of rice, ideally brown rice.

Did you know?
Edamame beans (also known as soya beans) are rich in phytonutrients.

Healthy Bolognese

I think it is important to keep to traditional family favourites, especially when dieting. Food is not just about taste, it is also about satisfying the mind.

1. Lightly spray your sauté pan with olive oil. Fry the onion and garlic over a medium/high heat until soft and translucent. Add the pepper and cook for another 5 minutes.

2. Add the mince and cook until brown. Add the mushrooms and cook for 2 more minutes.

3. Add the tinned tomatoes, red lentils and sundried tomato paste. Stir well. Add the grated carrot, stock, oregano and season with black pepper. Leave to simmer very gently for 20 minutes.

4. Serve on a bed of cooked spaghetti. If you are watching your weight, do not top with cheese!

Ingredients:

Olive oil spray

1 red onion, finely chopped

2–3 cloves garlic, finely chopped

1 pepper, finely chopped

350g turkey or quorn mince

50g mushrooms, finely chopped

1 tin chopped tomatoes

75g red lentils

2–3 tsp sundried tomato paste

1 carrot, grated

250ml vegetable or meat stock (or gluten-free stock)

1 tsp dried oregano

Black pepper

Wholemeal or low-carb spaghetti, or gluten-free

Nutritional information:

Hidden goodness – kids love it! Vegetarians can eat quorn, gluten-free

Healthy Turkey Burgers

Ingredients:

1 red onion, finely
   chopped

2 cloves garlic, crushed

1 stick celery, chopped

½ yellow pepper, chopped

300g turkey mince

30g pine nuts, crushed

1 tsp curry powder

1 tbsp home-prepared
   wholemeal breadcrumbs
   (or gluten-free)

Black pepper to taste

1 egg, beaten (optional)

Olive oil spray

Nutritional information:

Gluten-free

1. Place all the ingredients, except for the egg and olive oil, in a bowl and mix thoroughly.

2. When mixed, form into balls – these should be firm but moist. If the mixture is dry, add some beaten egg. Use the palm of your hand to flatten the balls into burger shapes. You can place them in the fridge until you are ready to use them, or freeze them in layers (separate each layer with parchment to prevent them sticking together).

3. When you are ready to cook the burgers, spray your sauté pan with olive oil. Cook the burgers over a medium/high heat (or grill them) for approximately 5 minutes on each side until golden.

4. Serve with wholemeal baps (or gluten-free), a salad garnish and a dollop of fat-free mayonnaise.

Did you know?

Lean turkey is a good source of protein, but also carnosine, which some research suggests could help slow down the aging process.

Chilli-stuffed Chicken

Serves
4

A very simple dish that takes minutes to prepare.

1. Preheat your oven to 200°C (Gas Mark 6).

2. Place the quark or yoghurt in a bowl and mix in the chilli and chilli powder until combined. Season to taste.

3. Using a sharp knife, cut a slit in each chicken breast to form a pocket. Stuff the pockets with the creamed mixture.

4. Place on a greased ovenproof dish. Spray with olive oil and season to taste.

5. Place in the oven and cook for 20–30 minutes until the chicken is cooked.

6. Serve with brown and wild rice and a green salad.

Ingredients:
4 lean chicken breasts (or turkey breasts)
2–4 tbsp quark or 0% fat Greek yoghurt
1–2 red chillies, finely chopped
½ tsp chilli powder
Seasoning
Olive oil spray

Nutritional information:
Gluten-free

Spring Chicken Casserole

Ingredients:

Olive oil spray

3–4 chicken breasts,
    skinless

250g new potatoes, finely
    sliced

1 carrot, finely diced

Bunch spring onions,
    chopped

450ml chicken stock,
    warmed (or gluten-free)

2 tsp paprika

Black pepper

Small handful fresh
    tarragon

Small handful fresh parsley

50g French beans

75g peas

Nutritional information:

Gluten-free, chicken is low
fat, rich in B3, B6,
selenium and phosphorus

This is the perfect dish to use up any of the lovely spring vegetables. Sometimes spring can still be a bit chilly so there is nothing better than a delicious, warming evening meal.

1. Spray your sauté pan with olive oil. Add the chicken and cook over a medium heat until it starts to brown. Add the sliced potatoes, carrot and spring onions and cook for another 5 minutes.

2. Add the stock, seasoning and herbs. Cover and simmer gently for 15 minutes.

3. Add the French beans and peas and cook for another 15 minutes.

4. Serve with sweet potato mash for a warming winter supper.

Chicken, Bacon and Bean Casserole

Serves
4–6

A very wholesome dish – perfect for filling a gap, especially on a winter's evening. The beans and lentils give you an extra protein boost, helping to bulk out the casserole and keeping you fuller for longer.

1. In a large sauté pan, add a spray of oil. Cook the onion, garlic and pepper over a medium/high heat for 5 minutes.

2. Add the chicken and cook until it turns white. Then add the bacon.

3. Add all remaining ingredients. Turn the heat to low and cook for 30–45 minutes.

4. This dish is quite substantial so you don't need to serve it with anything else.

Note: You can cook this in the slow cooker by adding all the ingredients and cooking for 4–6 hours.

Ingredients:

Olive oil spray
1 red onion, finely chopped
3 cloves garlic, roughly chopped
1 pepper, diced
400g lean, skinless chicken pieces (thigh gives more flavour)
4–5 rashers of lean back bacon – remove all fat
8 new potatoes, halved or quartered
1 large sweet potato, peeled and diced
2 carrots, diced
2 sticks celery, diced
1 tin chopped tomatoes
900ml chicken stock (or gluten-free)
75g red lentils
1 tin borlotti beans (or chickpeas)
2 tsp paprika
1 bay leaf
Black pepper
1 tsp dried tarragon

Nutritional information:
Gluten-free

Did you know?
Beans and lentils are packed with iron, zinc, magnesium and biotin.

Healthy Lamb Biryani

Ingredients:

Olive oil spray

450g lean lamb, cubed (if
you are really health
conscious, you could
swap lamb for quorn)

1 red onion, diced

2 cloves garlic, crushed

1 tsp ground cinnamon

1 tsp ground cardamom

½ tsp ground cloves

2–3 tsp curry powder

1 chilli, chopped (optional)

350ml plain 0% fat Greek
yoghurt

150ml lamb stock or
gluten-free

4 tomatoes, diced

250g brown basmati rice

Sprinkle of toasted
almonds

Nutritional information:

Gluten-free

Forget takeaways – make your own healthier and tastier versions
of your favourite dishes. You can make the lamb mixture in
advance and just cook the rice when you are ready to assemble.

1. In a sauté pan, heat a spray of oil over a medium/high heat
until hot. Add the lamb, onion and garlic and cook until the lamb
starts to brown and the onion starts to soften.

2. Add the spices and cook for a couple of minutes before adding
the yoghurt, stock and tomatoes. Combine well and gently cook
on a low heat for 10 minutes.

3. Meanwhile cook your rice as per the packet's instructions. I
normally add 1½ cups of water to 1 cup of rice, bring to the boil
and then leave it simmering for a couple of minutes before
popping a lid on and removing completely from the heat. Leave
to stand for 10–12 minutes and then fluff up using a fork.

4. When the rice is done, preheat your oven to 180°C (Gas Mark 4).

5. Place a layer of rice in the bottom of your ovenproof dish.
Follow this with a layer of the lamb mixture. Continue until you
have used up all the ingredients.

6. Cover with foil, place in the oven and cook for 15–20 minutes.

7. Garnish with toasted almonds before serving.

Ingredients:

Olive oil spray

1 large red onion, chopped

2–3 cloves garlic, crushed

400g lamb, diced

3–4 tsp harissa paste or
hot chilli paste

2 tsp ground cinnamon
powder

1–2 sweet potatoes,
peeled and diced

1 tin chopped tomatoes

1 tin chickpeas, drained

400ml water or stock (or
gluten-free)

100g dried apricots,
chopped

Fresh coriander leaves to
garnish

Nutritional information:

Gluten-free

Lamb, Chickpea and Apricot Casserole

This is a lovely and wholesome dish with a slight Moroccan feel. Perfect for filling you up on a winter's evening.

1. In a large casserole dish, add a spray of olive oil and cook the onion, garlic and lamb over a medium/high heat for 5 minutes.

2. Add the harissa paste and stir well for 3 minutes.

3. Add all remaining ingredients and cook slowly for 1 hour on your hob on a low heat. This recipe is perfect made in a slow cooker, giving really tender meat. Cook for 6–8 hours.

> **Did you know?**
> Dried apricots are a rich source of iron.

4. Garnish with coriander leaves before serving.

Chilli con Carne

1. Over a medium heat, spray a pan with a little olive oil. Add the onion and star anise and cook until the onion starts to soften.

2. Remove the star anise and add the garlic, pepper, celery and carrot and cook for 5 minutes, stirring regularly.

3. Add the chopped chillis, cook for 2 more minutes. then add the mince and cook until brown.

5. Add the tinned tomatoes. Fill half the tin with water and swirl around, and add this to the mince. Add the red kidney beans, mushrooms and remaining herbs and spices. Season to taste.

7. Allow to simmer gently for 20 minutes. The longer this is cooked, the thicker it will become. If it gets too thick, you can add more water.

8. Serve on a bed of rice (ideally brown for those who are health conscious), or use in wholemeal wraps, tortilla dishes or even as a topping for jacket potatoes.

Ingredients:

Olive oil spray

1 red onion, finely chopped

1 star anise

2 cloves garlic, crushed

1 red pepper, diced

1 stick celery, finely diced

1 carrot, finely diced

1–2 chopped chillis (depending on desired flavour)

400g lean beef mince (pre-drained of fat) or quorn mince

1 tin chopped tomatoes

1 tin red kidney beans

75g mushrooms, quartered (optional)

1–2 tsp chilli powder (depending on desired flavour)

1 tsp paprika

Seasoning

Handful of fresh coriander leaves

Nutritional information:

Gluten-free, vegetarian if quorn is used

Mustard Pork Loin Chops with Golden Mash

Olive oil spray

4 large loin pork chops, with all fat removed (if small, allow 2 per person)

1–2 tbsp wholegrain mustard

2–3 large potatoes, diced

2 sweet potatoes, diced

1 carrot, diced

6 tbsp low-fat crème fraîche or 0% fat-free natural yoghurt

Black pepper

Nutritional information:

Gluten-free

1. Preheat the oven to 190°C (Gas Mark 5).

2. Place the pork on a baking tray sprayed with a small amount of olive oil. Spread a layer of wholegrain mustard over each chop. Cover with foil and place in the oven. Cook for 20–25 minutes, or until cooked (the cooking time depends on the size of the chops). Meanwhile, steam or boil the potato, sweet potato and carrot until tender.

3. Drain and mash until smooth and then stir in the crème fraiche and season to taste.

4. Serve with green vegetables.

Bacon, Thyme and Rosemary Chicken Breasts

Serves

4

Use lean bacon for this recipe otherwise it can be high in fat. Serve with a selection of nutrient rich salads, or if you prefer a hot accompaniment, serve with sweet potato mash and steamed green vegetables.

1. Preheat the oven to 200°C (Gas Mark 6).

2. Prepare your chicken breasts. Using a sharp knife, cut a pocket in each breast ready to stuff.

3. Mix the garlic, herbs and quark together. Season to taste. Stuff each breast with the mixture.

4. Wrap each breast with the bacon. Place on a non-stick (or greased) baking tray, seam-side down.

5. Bake for 20–30 minutes, depending on the size of your chicken breasts. Test to see if they are cooked before serving.

Ingredients:

4 large skinless chicken breasts, with all fat removed

3 cloves garlic, crushed

2 tbsp parlsey, freshly chopped

Few sprigs rosemary, chopped

Few sprigs thyme, chopped

3–4 tbsp quark

Black pepper

4–8 rashers lean bacon

Nutritional information:

Gluten-free

Chicken Fricassée

Olive oil spray

800g chicken breast,
    chopped into chunks

2 large red onions, roughly
    chopped

3 cloves garlic, roughly
    chopped

2 peppers, thickly sliced

2 large carrots, cut into
    slices or thin batons

80g button mushrooms

400ml chicken stock
    (ideally homemade, if
    not use low-salt chicken
    stock and gluten-free if
    coeliac)

1 tsp paprika

½ tsp dried parsley

Few sprigs fresh thyme

2 bay leaves

Seasoning

Nutritional information:

Gluten-free

1. Preheat the oven to 190°C (Gas Mark 5).

2. Spray a large hob-proof casserole dish with olive oil. Place on your hob over a medium heat. Add the chicken and cook until it turns white.

3. Add all the remaining ingredients, stirring to ensure they are evenly distributed. Season to taste.

4. Place in the oven for 30–40 minutes, until the chicken is cooked. Serve immediately

Cowboy Pie

Kids love this variation on the cottage pie. The hidden sweet potato and carrots provide some extra goodness and the baked beans more protein for a fuller-for-longer feeling.

1. Place the potato, sweet potato and carrots in a steamer or boil until soft.

2. Meanwhile, spray a little oil in a large sauté pan and fry the onion over a medium heat for 3–4 minutes. Then add the mince and cook until brown.

3. Add the baked beans and chopped tomatoes and cook for 10 minutes until tender and reduced to the desired consistency. Season to taste and add a splash of Worcestershire sauce.

4. Preheat your oven to 180°C (Gas Mark 4).

5. Mash the steamed potato and carrots together. Add the skimmed milk, season to taste and mix thoroughly.

6. Place the mince in a deep ovenproof dish and spoon the mash over the top. Be careful not to overfill the dish. Press the mash down gently with a fork. Top with the grated cheese and a sprinkle of paprika.

7. Cook in the oven for 20–25 minutes until golden.

Ingredients:

2–3 large potatoes, chopped into rough chunks
2 sweet potatoes, chopped into chunks
1–2 carrots, chopped into chunks
Olive oil spray
1 red onion, chopped
500g quorn mince, lean beef mince (pre-drained of fat) or turkey mince
1 tin baked beans (ideally low-salt, low-sugar)
1 tin chopped tomatoes
Seasoning
Worcestershire sauce
50–100ml skimmed milk
25g low-fat mature Cheddar, grated
Paprika

Nutritional information:
Gluten-free

Left: Cowboy Pie

Turkey, Pepper and Tomato Pasta

Ingredients:

Olive oil spray

3–4 turkey breasts, cut
into chunks

1 small red onion, finely
chopped

2–3 cloves garlic, crushed

1–2 red peppers, sliced

100g button mushrooms,
whole or halved
(optional)

1 tin chopped tomatoes

2 tbsp sundried tomato
paste

Small handful basil leaves

Seasoning

300g whole-wheat or
gluten-free penne pasta

Nutritional information:

Gluten-free

A simple dish that takes less than 30 minutes to prepare. Turkey is lower in fat than chicken but, if you prefer, you can use lean chicken breasts.

1. In a sauté pan over a medium heat, spray a little olive oil. Add the turkey chunks and cook for 5–8 minutes.

2. Add the onion, garlic, peppers and mushrooms if you are using them. Cook for 5 more minutes before adding the tomatoes, sundried tomato paste, basil leaves and seasoning. Leave on a low heat to simmer gently.

3. Meanwhile, add the pasta to boiling water and cook as per the packet's instructions.

4. Drain the pasta and add to the turkey mixture, stirring well to ensure it is well combined. Season to taste before serving.

Garlic and Chilli Lamb Chops

1. In a blender, whizz the chilli, garlic, lime and olive oil. Season to taste. Pour over the lamp chops and leave to marinate for 2 hours.

2. When you are ready to cook, place the chops on your grill pan and grill on a medium/high heat for 6–8 minutes on both sides.

3. Serve with new potatoes and green vegetables.

Did you know?

Chillies contain a chemical called capsaicin, which raises the body temperature. A recent study found that eating around 1g a day can help you burn off more calories. Those eating chillies were also found to consume less food as they felt less hungry, and had fewer cravings for fatty, salty or sugary foods.

Ingredients:

2–3 chillies

4 cloves garlic

Zest of ½ lime

2 tbsp olive oil

Black pepper

Sea salt

8 lamb chops, with fat
    removed

Nutritional information:

Gluten-free

Roasted One-pot Chicken with Sweet Potato and Squash

Ingredients:

2 large red onions, cut
    into wedges

4 cloves garlic, left whole

1 chilli, finely sliced

3 sweet potatoes, with
    skins left on, chopped
    into thick chunks

1 small squash, with skin
    left on, chopped into
    chunks

Spray of olive oil or drizzle
    of chilli oil

4 tsp paprika

Black pepper

4 chicken breasts

12 cherry tomatoes

Nutritional information:

Gluten-free, rich in
antioxidants

Roasted sweet potato and squash have a fantastic flavour – add some garlic and chilli and you have a divine meal. Feel free to add more chilli to taste or, for extra flavour, use chilli oil instead of olive oil.

1. Preheat the oven to 200°C (Gas Mark 6).

2. Place the onion, garlic, chilli, sweet potato and squash in your roasting tin and spray with olive oil. Toss well and spray again if needed. Sprinkle with 2 tsp paprika and season with black pepper.

3. Place in the oven and cook for 10 minutes.

4. Add the chicken and cherry tomatoes. Spray again with olive oil and sprinkle with the remaining paprika.

5. Bake for another 20–25 minutes until the chicken is cooked.

6. Serve with a green salad.

Cajun Chicken with Spicy Salsa

This is a great meal. Leave the chicken to marinate for an hour or two to enhance the flavour. You can prepare both the chicken and the salsa in advance. Quick and easy!

1. Take your chicken breasts and flatten them.

2. Mix the spices together in a bowl. Spray the chicken with olive oil and then rub the spice mixture into the flesh. Leave to one side for at least 20 minutes, ideally 1–2 hours.

3. Meanwhile, prepare the remaining vegetables and place in a bowl. Mix together with the coriander and chilli. Stir in the lime zest and juice, olive oil and balsamic vinegar. Add more to taste if needed.

4. When you are ready to cook the chicken, heat a griddle over a high heat. Add the chicken, cooking for 5–6 minutes each side until done.

5. Serve on a bed of the salsa.

Ingredients:

4 chicken breasts
2 tsp ground cumin
2 tsp ground coriander
2 tsp chilli powder
2 tsp paprika
Olive oil spray
½ cucumber, diced
1 red onion, diced
4–6 spring onions, sliced,
   including the green
   stalks
1 red pepper, diced
1 yellow pepper, diced
10 cherry tomatoes,
   halved
1 small handful fresh
   coriander, chopped
1 chilli, finely diced
Zest and juice of ½ lime
2 tbsp olive oil
2 tsp balsamic vinegar

Nutritional information:
Gluten-free

Ingredients:

300g wholemeal, low-carb
  or gluten-free spaghetti
Olive oil spray
1 small red onion, finely
  chopped
2 cloves garlic, crushed
100g pancetta or, to be
  extra healthy, very lean
  bacon or ham
75g parmesan, freshly
  grated (or use low fat
  mature Cheddar)
3 large eggs
150ml fat-free Greek
  yoghurt
Seasoning

Nutritional information:

Gluten-free

Healthy Carbonara

Forget the high-fat, cream-rich carbonara – this recipe uses a
more traditional recipe, with a healthy adaption of course!
Parmesan is high in fat though, so you could substitute a low fat
mature cheddar if you prefer.

1. Cook the spaghetti in a pan as per the packet's instructions.

2. Meanwhile, spray a sauté pan with a little olive oil and place
over a medium heat. Add the onion, garlic and pancetta and cook
until they soften and the pancetta starts to go a bit crispy.

3. In a bowl mix the cheese, eggs and yoghurt and season to taste.

4. Drain the spaghetti. Add the pancetta mixture and combine
well. Add the egg mix and stir. The heat of the spaghetti will cook
the eggs resulting in a creamy sauce.

5. Serve immediately.

Paprika Chicken

I use red onions in my recipes as they have a higher nutrient content than other onions. There have been suggestions that red onions also have cancer fighting benefits (as has green tea, turmeric, garlic and broccoli). Onions also contain allicin, which helps fight disease and can help lower blood pressure.

1. Spray a little olive oil in your sauté pan. Add the onion and pepper and cook over a medium heat until they start to soften.

2. Add the chicken pieces and brown.

3. Add the paprika and chicken stock and allow to simmer gently for 10–15 minutes.

4. Stir in the crème fraîche.

5. Sprinkle with chopped parsley before serving with brown rice and vegetables.

Ingredients:

Olive oil spray

2 red onions, finely chopped

1 red pepper, sliced

500g chicken, diced (breast or thigh are fine but remove any fat or skin) or use quorn pieces

2–3 tbsp smoked paprika

300ml chicken stock (or gluten-free)

150ml low-fat crème fraîche

Parsley, chopped, to serve

Nutritional information:

Gluten-free

Chapter 9
Fish

We should all eat more oily fish. Packed with essential omega-3, oily fish should be included in at least three meals a week. Choose from mackerel, trout, salmon, sardines, pilchards and herring. If you don't like oily fish, why not consider taking a daily supplement, but buy one from a good company such as Nutrigold, Solgar or Patrick Holford. Cod liver oil is not the same as omega-3 rich fish oil – don't buy it. I am really impressed with the new krill oil. Research shows that it provides substantially greater reduction of fat in the heart and liver than omega-3 from fish oil, whilst also helping reduce high blood pressure, lower cholesterol and it could even protect against osteoporosis. It has been noted to help reduce wrinkles – my kind of supplement!

Baked Coley, Fennel and Red Onion

Fennel features prominently in Mediterranean cuisine. It is delicious with fish. You could use cod or pollack in this recipe if you prefer.

1. Preheat your oven to 200°C (Gas Mark 6).

2. Prepare your fish fillets. Season well and squeeze with a little lemon juice. Leave to one side until needed.

3. Place the sliced fennel, onion, garlic and 1 lemon, cut into wedges, in a roasting or baking tray.

4. Spray with olive oil and place in the oven for 15 minutes.

5. Place the fish fillets on top of the vegetables. Squeeze the juice of 1 lemon and drizzle over the dish. Season to taste. Cover securely with foil. Bake for another 15–20 minutes until the fish is thoroughly cooked and flakes easily off the fork.

6. Remove from the foil and serve with steamed new potatoes and a fresh green salad.

Ingredients:

2–4 coley fish fillets

Seasoning

2 lemons

1 large or 2 small bulbs fennel, sliced

2 red onions, sliced

2–3 cloves garlic, finely sliced

Olive oil spray

Nutritional information:

Gluten-free

Did you know?
Oily fish has been shown to help protect you from Alzheimer's.

Foil-baked Salmon with Mango Salsa

Ingredients:

4 salmon fillets

1 lemon, sliced

1 lemon, for juice

Seasoning

1 ripe mango

1 ripe avocado

1 red chilli, finely chopped

6 spring onions, finely
   chopped

1 yellow pepper, diced

Zest and juice of ½ lime

Generous handful of
   rocket, lamb's leaf,
   watercress or mixed leaf
   salad leaves for each
   serving

½ cucumber, diced

Small handful of coriander,
   chopped

½ lime to serve

Nutritional information:

Gluten-free, rich in
omega-3

1. Preheat the oven to 190°C (Gas Mark 5).

2. Place each salmon fillet in the centre of a piece of foil. Add 1 or 2 slices of lemon on top. Finish with a squeeze of extra lemon juice and season to taste. Wrap and place on a baking tray. Place in the oven and cook for 15–20 minutes or until cooked to your own personal taste.

3. Meanwhile place all remaining ingredients, apart from the salad leaves, cucumber and coriander, together in a bowl and mash/mix well.

4. Just prior to serving, place salad leaves and coriander on a serving plate. Place the salmon on the top and drizzle with salsa. Serve with the remaining salsa and half lime to the side.

Did you know?

Oily fish is not only rich in omega-3, it is also a good source of vitamin A – a potent antioxidant.

Salmon Fish Cakes

1. Mix the fish, potato, spring onions, lemon juice and herbs together in a bowl. Season to taste. Add the egg to bind if needed.

2. Form the mixture into cakes, place on baking parchment and chill in the fridge for 10 minutes.

3. Remove from the fridge, brush with a light coating of olive oil and grill both sides until browned. Alternatively, you can spray your sauté pan with olive oil, and fry gently until browned each side.

4. Serve with new potatoes and green salad.

Ingredients:

400g fresh or tinned
   salmon
300g potatoes, cooked
   and mashed
3–4 spring onions, very
   finely chopped
Juice of ½ lemon
2–3 tsp fresh dill
2–3 tsp tarragon
Black pepper
1 egg, beaten
Olive oil or olive oil spray

Nutritional information:
Gluten-free, rich in
omega-3

Baked Salmon with Minted Salsa and Roasted Tomatoes

Serves
4

Salmon is rich in omega 3, is a good source of protein and packed with vitamins, minerals and micronutrients.

1. Preheat the oven to 190°C (Gas Mark 5).

2. Place each salmon fillet in the centre of a piece of foil. Add 1 or 2 slices of lemon on top. Finish with a squeeze of extra lemon juice and season to taste. Wrap and place on a baking tray.

3. Place the tomatoes on a baking tray, keeping their stalks intact. Drizzle with a little olive oil, sprinkle with sea salt and black pepper.

4. Place the salmon in the oven and cook for 15–20 minutes or until cooked to your own personal taste.

5. Add the tomatoes, 10–12 minutes before the salmon should be cooked.

6. Meanwhile, place all remaining ingredients apart from the extra virgin olive oil together in a bowl and mix well. Then drizzle with olive oil.

7. Place the salmon on a serving plate with the baked tomatoes. Top with the salsa and finish with a drizzle of extra virgin olive oil and a few mint leaves. Serve with a lime wedge to the side.

Ingredients:

4 salmon fillets
1 lemon, sliced
1 lemon, for juice
Sea salt
Black pepper
12 vine tomatoes
Olive oil
1 red onion, diced
1 ripe avocado, diced
1 red chilli, finely chopped
1 red pepper, diced
Zest and juice of 1 lime
½ cucumber, diced
Small handful mint leaves, chopped
Extra virgin olive oil
Extra lime to serve
Extra mint leaves to serve

Nutritional information:

Gluten-free, rich in omega 3

Wholemeal Breaded Fish Fillets

Ingredients:

50g home-prepared
   wholemeal breadcrumbs
   (or gluten-free)
1 tbsp oats (or gluten-
   free)
1 tbsp chives
1 tbsp parsley
1 tbsp parmesan cheese,
   grated
Zest of 1 lemon
4 fish fillets
4–5 tsp low-fat cream
   cheese

Nutritional information:

Gluten-free

You can use any fish fillet for this. Speak to your fishmonger for the best deals. Remember to opt for omega-3 rich fish if you can.

1. Preheat the oven to 180°C (Gas Mark 4).

2. Place the breadcrumbs, oats, chives, parsley, parmesan and lemon zest in a bowl and combine well.

3. Cover the fillets in cream cheese. (Just the top or it will get too messy!)

4. Dip into the breaded mixture, ensuring they are well covered, and then place on a greased/lined baking tray.

5. Bake in the oven for 10–15 minutes.

6. Serve with salad and new potatoes.

Mackerel Pâté

This is a very easy recipe to follow and can be prepared in seconds.

1. Make sure your mackerel fillets are free from bones and skin. If you are not sure about this, ask your fishmonger to do it for you.

2. Place all ingredients in a liquidiser or small food processor. Whizz for a few seconds until the ingredients have blended well. Season to taste.

3. Allow the pâté to settle for at least 20 minutes for the flavours to infuse before serving.

Ingredients:

4 mackerel fillets, boned and cooked
1 small tub low-fat cream cheese
Zest and juice of 1 lemon
Handful of fresh parsley, chopped
Seasoning

Nutritional information:

Gluten-free, rich in omega-3

Did you know?

Mackerel is rich in omega-3 and it also contains B12 which regulates the functioning of our brain and nervous system. It is also a good source of selenium which helps fight free radial damage. Avoid smoked mackerel as it is high in salt.

Lemon and Ginger Mackerel Salad

Ingredients:

5cm knuckle ginger,
    grated

Zest and juice of 1 large
    lemon

2 cloves garlic, crushed

1 tbsp olive oil

Black pepper

4 mackerel fillets

125g mixed green salad
    leaves (e.g. rocket,
    watercress, spinach,
    lamb's lettuce, chard,
    radicchio, curly endive)

2 carrots, grated

12–16 cherry tomatoes,
    quartered

Small handful of sugar
    snap peas, cut into 3

½ cucumber, diced

Nutritional information:

Gluten-free, rich in
omega-3

1. Mix the ginger, lemon, garlic and olive oil together. Season to
taste with black pepper.

2. With a sharp knife, lightly score the skin of each mackerel fillet.
Rub the ginger mixture over the top, paying particular attention
to the scored areas.

3. Place the mackerel under a preheated grill and cook on both
sides for 3–4 minutes.

4. Meanwhile, place some washed leaves on each plate. Top with
carrot, cherry tomatoes, sugar snap peas and cucumber. Combine
well.

5. Place the fish on top of each salad. Drizzle any remaining
ginger dressing over the fillets before serving.

Sweetcorn, Cherry Tomato and Tuna Pasta

1. Place the pasta in a pan of boiling water and cook as per the packet's instructions.

2. Meanwhile, spray your sauté pan with a little olive oil. Add the onion and garlic (if using) and cook on a medium heat until soft. Add the tuna and sweetcorn and stir well. Then turn off the heat. Add the milk and the cream cheese and put a lid on the pan to retain the heat. It will start to melt together.

3. Drain the pasta and then return the pasta to the saucepan. Add the tuna mix and the cherry tomatoes. Season to taste and sprinkle with some fresh herbs.

4. Mix well for a couple of minutes over the heat of the hob that was used for boiling the pasta. If using a gas hob you will need the heat on low.

5. Serve immediately

Ingredients:

300g dried wholemeal or low-carb pasta (or gluten-free)
Olive oil spray
1 red onion, finely chopped
2 cloves garlic (optional)
1 tin tuna, drained
1 small tin sweetcorn or 125g frozen sweetcorn, defrosted
200ml skimmed milk
200g low-fat cream cheese
12 cherry tomatoes, halved or quartered
Seasoning
Small handful of fresh herbs (e.g. parsley, basil or oregano)

Nutritional information:
Gluten-free

Pollack and Vegetable Tagine

You can use pollack, coley or sustainable cod for this recipe.

Ingredients:

500g pollack fillets, cut
   into large chunks
Black pepper
3 tbsp olive oil
Juice and zest of ½ lemon
1 small handful of
   coriander leaves
3–4 cloves garlic
1 chilli
1 tsp cumin
1 tsp ground coriander
3 tsp paprika
Olive oil spray
1 large red onion
1 red pepper, sliced
1 yellow pepper, sliced
300g new potatoes,
   halved
2 sweet potatoes, thickly
   diced
1 tin chopped tomatoes
1 tin chickpeas, drained
250ml fish stock (or
   gluten-free)
Coriander to serve

Nutritional information:

Gluten-free

1. Place the fillet chunks in a bowl. Season with black pepper.

2. In a blender, mix the oil, lemon zest and juice, coriander leaves, garlic, chilli, cumin, ground coriander and paprika. Whizz until smooth.

3. Pour this over the fish, cover with cling film and leave to marinate in the fridge for at least 2 hours or overnight if you prefer.

4. When you are ready to cook, use a large stock pot. Spray with a little olive oil before adding the onion and peppers. Cook on your hob over a medium heat until they start to soften.

5. Add the fish, including all of the marinade. Cook for another 5 minutes.

6. Add all the remaining ingredients. Allow to simmer gently, then pop on the lid and cook on a low/medium heat for 35–45 minutes.

7. Garnish with a few sprigs of coriander and you could serve this in a tagine.

Mackerel Salad

Ingredients:

1 tin mackerel or 4 fillets,
   boned, cooked and cut
   into chunks
6–8 cherry tomatoes,
   halved
½ cucumber, diced
4–6 spring onions, chopped
Handful of basil leaves,
   lightly torn
Seasoning
125g mixed green salad
   leaves (e.g. rocket,
   watercress, spinach,
   lamb's lettuce, chard,
   radicchio, curly endive)
3 hard-boiled eggs, halved
Extra basil leaves to sprinkle

Dressing
50ml olive oil
20ml balsamic vinegar
Lemon juice to taste
Black pepper
Sea salt
Dijon mustard (optional)
Fresh herbs e.g. oregano
   (optional)

Nutritional information:

Gluten-free, rich in
omega-3, vitamins D and
B12, selenium and
phosphorus

You can use fresh or tinned mackerel for this recipe. If you use fresh mackerel, cook it in a shallow pan for 3–4 minutes each side or as instructed by your fishmonger.

1. Place the mackerel chunks in a bowl and mix with the cherry tomatoes, cucumber, spring onions and basil and season to taste.

2. Line a large serving dish with a bed of mixed green salad leaves. Add the mackerel mix and cover with the eggs. Sprinkle with the remaining basil leaves.

3. Make the dressing by mixing the olive oil with the balsamic vinegar. Add lemon juice to taste and season with black pepper and sea salt. Taste as you go. You can also add a touch of Dijon mustard or some fresh herbs such as oregano. Drizzle the dressing over the salad.

Baked Salmon with New Potato Salad and Yoghurt Dressing

This dish can be prepared in advance.

1. Preheat the oven to 190°C (Gas Mark 5).

2. Place each fillet on a square of foil, drizzle with lemon juice, scatter with lemon zest and season with black pepper.

3. Seal the parcels, place on a baking tray and cook in the oven for 15–20 minutes or until cooked to your own personal taste.

4. Meanwhile, steam the potatoes until just soft.

5. Remove and add the spring onion and chives. Combine well and season to taste.

6. In a bowl mix the yoghurt, lemon juice, parsley and season.

7. Mix some of the yoghurt dressing with the potatoes, leaving some to pour onto the salmon.

8. Place the potatoes on each plate, top with a few slices of cucumber, followed by the salmon. Drizzle with the remaining yoghurt dressing. Serve with a leafy salad.

Ingredients:

4 salmon fillets
Zest and juice of 1 lemon
Black pepper
1kg new potatoes, halved
Small bunch spring onions, finely chopped
Small bunch chives, finely chopped
150g fat-free Greek yoghurt
1–2 tbsp lemon juice
Handful of chopped parsley
¼ cucumber, finely sliced

Nutritional information:

Gluten-free, rich in omega-3

Serves

4

Ingredients:

300g gluten-free rice and
vegetable pasta

50g pitted olives, halved

12 cherry tomatoes,
halved

1 red onion, finely
chopped

400g tin tuna, drained

Black pepper

Nutritional information:

Gluten-free

Tuna, Olive and Tomato Pasta Salad

This is a versatile recipe that can be served hot or cold.

1. Cook the pasta as per the packet's instructions.

2. Meanwhile, place all the remaining ingredients in a bowl and combine. Season to taste with black pepper.

3. Drain the pasta and combine with the vegetables.

4. Serve immediately or cold as a salad.

Baked Pesto Fish

I have chosen coley for this dish, but you can choose any similar fish fillet, such as cod or pollack. Speak to you fishmonger for more suggestions.

1. Preheat the oven to 200°C (Gas Mark 6).

2. Place each fillet on a square of baking parchment or foil, large enough to secure.

3. Cover the fillets with a layer of pesto. Drizzle with olive oil and season with black pepper.

4. Seal the parcels and place on a baking tray. Place in the oven and cook for 15–20 minutes until the fish is tender and flaking.

5. Serve with new potatoes and green vegetables.

Ingredients:

4 fish fillets (e.g. coley,
   cod or pollack)
2–3 tbsp pesto
Olive oil
Black pepper

Nutritional information:

Gluten-free

Chapter 10
Vegetarian

I am a big fan of vegetarian meals, partly because I was a vegetarian for over 20 years, but also for health reasons. It is good to have at least two vegetarian main meals a week. Try to avoid too much dairy – I know it is hard as many vegetarians rely so much on cheese to make their meals special. Get to know the flavours of vegetables, pulses, beans and herbs. You will find you digest vegetarian meals easier than meat dishes. Remember, for all those who feel they miss the texture of meat quorn is an excellent meat substitute. It is low fat, high in protein and often people cannot tell the difference, particularly when using the mince.

Spicy Tofu Burgers

Serves
4–6

Tofu is made from soya beans. It is a great source of phytonutrients (being shown to aid in balancing hormones, especially during menopause). It is also an excellent source of protein, so ideal for vegetarians and vegans or those wanting to avoid the health dangers of eating too much red meat. It has also been shown to help lower cholesterol. It is quite bland on its own but does absorb other flavours well.

1. In a large bowl, place the chickpeas and mash until soft. Add the tofu and continue to mash until mixed thoroughly.

2. Meanwhile, spray a pan with olive oil. Over a medium heat fry the onion, garlic, chilli and celery until soft. Add to the chickpea and tofu mixture.

3. Add the tomato purée, garam masala, soy sauce and seasoning. Stir well and then add the breadcrumbs and oats.

4. Mix thoroughly and form into balls (using a floured surface if the mixture is sticky). They should be firm but moist. Then use the palm of your hand to flatten them into burger shapes.

5. Place the burgers in the fridge until ready to use or freeze them. (Line with parchment to prevent them from sticking together.)

6. When you are ready to cook, grill or lightly fry the burgers in olive oil. Cook for 4–5 minutes on each side until golden.

7. Serve with wholemeal baps (or gluten-free), garnished with salad.

Ingredients:

1 tin chickpeas, drained
250g or 1 pack firm tofu
Olive oil spray
1 onion, finely chopped
1–2 cloves garlic, crushed
1 chilli, finely chopped
1 stick celery, finely chopped
1 tsp tomato purée
1 tsp garam masala
Splash of soy sauce
Seasoning
1 tbsp home-prepared wholemeal breadcrumbs (or gluten-free)
1 tbsp oats (or gluten free)

Nutritional information:
Vegetarian, vegan, gluten-free

Chickpea and Cashew Nut Burgers

Ingredients:

1 tbsp home-prepared
  wholemeal breadcrumbs
1 tbsp oats
400g cooked chickpeas (or
  1 tin, drained)
1–2 cloves garlic, crushed
1 onion, finely chopped
1 large or 2 medium
  carrots, grated
2 tbsp tomato purée
100g cashew nuts,
  chopped
1 egg
2–3 tsp Worcestershire
  sauce (opt for the
  vegetarian version)
Seasoning
Olive oil (optional)

Nutritional information:

Vegetarian

These aren't just for vegetarians! I had a barbeque last summer and these were devoured by the meat eaters as well as the vegetarians. If you like a spicy nut burger, you could add some chopped chillies, chilli powder or curry powder to the mixture.

1. In a small bowl, mix the breadcrumbs and oats together and leave to one side.

2. Mash the chickpeas until broken up and softened in a large mixing bowl. Add the garlic, onion and carrots and stir well.

3. Add the tomato purée and mix thoroughly before adding the cashew nuts.

4. Add the egg, Worcestershire sauce and seasoning.

5. Mix thoroughly and form into balls, which should be firm but moist. If the mixture is too wet, add a sprinkle of oats. If too dry, add a small amount of olive oil.

6. Use the palm of your hand to flatten the balls into burger shapes. Then dip each one into the breadcrumb mixture.

7. Place the burgers into the fridge until ready to use or freeze them. (Line with parchment to prevent them from sticking together.)

8. When you are ready to cook, grill or lightly fry the burgers in olive oil. Cook for 4–5 minutes on each side until golden.

9. Serve with wholemeal baps, garnished with salad.

Healthy Moussaka

1. Preheat the oven to 190°C (Gas Mark 5).

2. In a pan of boiling water, add the sliced aubergines for 2 minutes. Then remove and pat dry. Leave to one side.

3. Meanwhile, in a sauté pan cook the onion and garlic in a little olive oil over a medium heat. Add the mince and cook for another 5 minutes.

4. Add the tomatoes and purée, mint and cinnamon and simmer gently for 10 minutes.

5. Place a layer of mince in an ovenproof dish, followed by a layer of aubergine. Finish with a layer of mince.

6. Finally, mix the crème fraîche with the grated cheese and pour over the final layer of mince.

7. Garnish with a sprinkle of parmesan before placing in the oven for 30–40 minutes.

Ingredients:

2–3 aubergines, sliced

Olive oil

1 red onion, chopped

2 cloves garlic, crushed

400g quorn mince

1 tin chopped tomatoes

2 tsp tomato purée

1 tsp dried mint

2 tsp cinnamon powder

300ml low-fat crème
    fraîche or fat-free Greek
    yoghurt

30g mature cheddar or
    parmesan cheese, grated

Seasoning

Nutritional information:

Vegetarian, gluten-free

Lentil Dahl

Ingredients:

Olive oil

1 red onion, chopped

2 cloves garlic, crushed

2½–5cm knuckle fresh
  ginger

1 pepper, chopped
  (optional)

2 tbsp mild/medium or
  sweet curry powder
  (mild is ideal for
  children)

1–2 tsp turmeric

1–2 tomatoes, finely
  chopped

1 tsp tomato purée

100g red lentils

300–400ml water

Coconut and a few sprigs
  of coriander to serve

Nutritional information:

Vegetarian, vegan, gluten-
free

I have had so much positive feedback about this recipe, I have included it here. Lentils are high in magnesium, low in fat and a good protein source. This is so easy to make and costs very little. You can make it mild and creamy by adding some fat-free Greek yoghurt, making it ideal for children, or spice it up to suit your taste.

1. In a large pan heat a little olive oil over a medium heat and fry the onion, garlic, ginger and pepper until soft.

2. Add the curry powder, turmeric, chopped tomatoes and tomato purée and cook for another 2 minutes.

3. Add the lentils and cover with water. Simmer gently until cooked. Add more water if necessary.

4. Sprinkle with coconut and garnish with coriander before serving.

Quorn and Spinach Curry

Ingredients:

Olive oil spray

1 large red onion, diced

1 pepper, diced

2 cloves garlic, crushed

1 tsp ginger, grated

1 chilli, finely chopped

500g quorn chunks

2 tbsp medium curry
    powder

1 400g tin chopped
    tomatoes

150ml water or vegetable
    stock (or gluten-free)

100g quartered
    mushrooms or baby
    mushrooms

400g baby spinach leaves

Small handful of coriander
    leaves, chopped

Seasoning

Nutritional information:

Vegetarian, gluten-free

Quorn is a fantastic, low-fat food, mainly used by vegetarians
(though not suitable for vegans). But it is a great food for
everyone and a cheaper, healthier alternative to meat.

1. Spray your sauté pan with a little olive oil and place on the hob
over a medium heat. Add the onion and pepper and sauté gently
for about 5 minutes until soft.

2. Add the garlic, ginger, chilli, quorn and curry powder and cook
for about 5 minutes.

3. Add the tomatoes, water/stock and mushrooms. Allow to
simmer very gently for 10–15 minutes.

4. Place the spinach and coriander on top of the mixture and
allow to wilt before stirring in completely. Season to taste.

5. Serve with brown or Basmati rice.

Quorn Meatball Hotpot

This is one of my sons favourite dishes. You can use lean beef mince or turkey mince for the meatballs, but quorn is low in fat and tastes good, plus they have the advantage of being ready made!

1. Place the new potatoes in a pan to steam or boil (steaming is healthier).

2. While the potatoes are steaming, spray a little olive oil in a sauté pan. Add the onion, garlic and pepper. Cook over a medium/high heat until they start to soften.

3. Add the chopped tomatoes. Fill the empty tomato tin half full of water and add this to the sauté pan. Add the thyme, black pepper and meatballs. Simmer gently for 10 minutes.

4. Preheat the oven to 180°C (Gas Mark 4).

5. When the potatoes are almost cooked, remove them from the pan.

6. In a casserole dish, place a layer of potatoes at the base. Add the meatball mixture and finish with a layer of potatoes. Season and cover with the cheese.

7. Place in the oven and cook for 15 minutes until golden.

8. Serve immediately.

Ingredients:

1kg new potatoes, quartered
Olive oil spray
1 red onion, sliced
2 cloves garlic, crushed
1 red pepper, diced
1 tin chopped tomatoes
1 tbsp fresh thyme, chopped
Black pepper
1 pack quorn meatballs
50g low-fat mature cheddar, grated

Nutritional information:

Vegetarian, gluten-free

Tomato, Olive and Basil Spaghetti

Ingredients:

300g wholemeal spaghetti
(or low-carb or gluten-
free)

Olive oil spray

1 red onion, finely
chopped

3 cloves garlic, finely
chopped

1 red or orange pepper,
finely chopped

6–8 tomatoes, chopped
(or 1 tin chopped
tomatoes)

1 tbsp sundried tomato
purée

Handful of olives, halved
and stoned

Handful of basil leaves,
freshly chopped

Extra basil to granish

Nutritional information:

Vegetarian, vegan, gluten-
free

1. Place the spaghetti in a pan of boiling water and cook as per the packet's instructions.

2. Meanwhile, add a spray of olive oil, the onion, garlic and pepper to a sauté pan and cook over a medium heat until they start to soften.

3. Add the tomatoes, tomato purée, olives and basil leaves. Cook for another few minutes.

4. Drain the spaghetti and add to the tomato mixture. Toss well ensuring the pasta is evenly coated.

5. Serve immediately with a garnish of basil leaves.

Quorn Bolognaise Stuffed Tomatoes

Perfect for using up any leftover bolognaise or why not double up the bolognaise part of the recipe below and use it to make two dishes at the same time.

1. Spray a sauté pan with a little olive oil. Add the onion, garlic and pepper and cook over a medium heat until they start to soften.

2. Add the quorn and cook for 5 minutes before adding the mushrooms, tomatoes, tomato purée and wine.

3. Season to taste and add the oregano and basil.

4. Leave to simmer gently for 10 minutes. Add a little water if it starts to dry up.

5. Meanwhile, preheat the oven to 190°C (Gas Mark 5).

6. Cut the tops off the beef tomatoes, keeping them to use as lids. Scoop out the centre of each tomato, chop and add to your bolognaise mixture. You will then be left with tomato shells and lids.

7. When the bolognaise mixture is ready, carefully fill the tomatoes without overfilling. Place the lids on top and place the tomatoes on a baking tray.

8. Spray with olive oil and season with sea salt and black pepper.

9. Place in the oven and bake for 15–20 minutes.

10. Serve immediately with a lovely salad.

Ingredients:

Olive oil spray
1 red onion, finely
   chopped
1–3 cloves garlic, crushed
   (depending on personal
   taste)
1 red pepper, diced
1 300g bag quorn mince
50g mushrooms, chopped
1 tin chopped tomatoes
2 tbsp sundried tomato
   purée
200ml low-calorie red wine
Sea salt
Black pepper
1 tsp dried oregano
Few basil leaves (optional)
8 beef tomatoes (extra
   large tomatoes)

Nutritional information:

Vegetarian, gluten-free

Mushroom and Cashew Nut Roast

Ingredients:

Spray olive oil

1 red onion, finely
chopped

200g cashew nuts,
chopped

250g mushrooms (I prefer
chestnut but choose
whatever works for you),
chopped

2 tsp yeast extract

50g wholemeal or gluten-
free breadcrumbs

Nutritional information:

Vegetarian, vegan, gluten-
free

This is made so much easier if you have a food processor that chops food. With mine, I can make this in minutes; otherwise you will drive yourself nuts (excuse the pun!) with all the chopping. I have many friends who are meat eaters and they all love this recipe.

1. Preheat the oven to 190°C (Gas Mark 5).

2. Spray a sauté pan with a little olive oil and cook the onion over a medium heat until translucent.

3. Add the nuts and mushrooms and cook for 5 minutes.

4. Add the yeast extract followed by the breadcrumbs and cook for another few minutes.

5. Place into a lined loaf tin and press down to form a firm base.

6. Bake in the oven for 30 minutes.

7. To add more pizzazz, why not serve with some roasted nuts on top.

Note: This can be frozen (before baking) and used when needed.

Spinach and Feta Pie

Serve this pie with a selection of fresh salad dishes and new potatoes – the perfect dish for a summer's evening.

1. Preheat the oven to 200°C (Gas Mark 6).

2. Melt the margarine in a saucepan or microwave.

3. Layer 3 sheets of filo pastry in the base of your pie dish. Brush margarine between each sheet and allow them to hang over the edge of the dish so that you can use them to form the sides of the pie.

4. Place a thin layer of spinach leaves, then a layer of crumbled feta and season with black pepper. Repeat this, finishing with a feta layer. Sprinkle over a little nutmeg.

5. Bring the edges of the pastry up and over the top of the pie. Cover with more filo sheets where necessary by simply crunching up filo and placing in the gaps, again brushing the filo with margarine. Sprinkle with sesame or poppy seeds.

6. Place in the oven and bake for 30–40 minutes, until golden.

7. Serve hot or cold.

Ingredients:

40g Pure or low-fat
   margarine
6 sheets filo pastry
400g baby leaf spinach,
   roughly torn
250g low-fat feta cheese,
   crumbled
Black pepper
¼ tsp nutmeg
Sesame or poppy seeds

Nutritional information:

Vegetarian

Vegetable Crumble

Ingredients:

1 red onion, finely
chopped

2–3 cloves garlic, roughly
chopped

1 red pepper, sliced

1 green pepper, sliced

2 courgettes, sliced

½ aubergine, diced

1 sweet potato, diced

Olive oil spray

2–3 sprigs of thyme

75g wholemeal flour

25g Pure or low-fat
margarine

40g oats

30g wholemeal
breadcrumbs

25g peanuts, chopped

25g sunflower seeds

25g pumpkin seed

2 tbsp linseeds

Seasoning

1 tin chopped tomatoes

1 tin butterbeans, drained

150ml water or low-salt
vegetable stock

Nutritional information:

Vegetarian

This can be prepared in advance or frozen uncooked, ready to cook when needed.

1. Preheat the oven to 200°C (Gas Mark 6).

2. Chop all the vegetables and place on a baking tray. Spray with a little olive oil and add a few sprigs of thyme.

3. Bake in the oven for 20 minutes.

4. Meanwhile, you can prepare the crumble. Rub the flour with the Pure or margarine to form breadcrumbs.

5. Mix in the oats, breadcrumbs, peanuts and seeds. Season to taste and leave to one side.

6. Remove the roasted vegetables from the oven. Place in your ovenproof dish, and stir in the chopped tomatoes, drained butterbeans and water or stock. Season to taste.

7. Cover with the crumble mix.

8. Place back in the oven, turning it down to 180°C (Gas Mark 4) and cook for 15–20 minutes.

9. Serve with a salad.

Right: Tomato, Rocket and Goat's Cheese Tart

Tomato, Rocket and Goat's Cheese Tart

Serves
1–2

A simple dish, created when I was hungry and needed to use up some home-grown tomatoes. I love the flavours of tomatoes, rocket and goat's cheese – though if you are watching your weight, don't overload the cheese!

1. Place the tortilla on a baking tray. Cover with a thin layer of sundried tomato paste.

2. Cover with the cherry tomatoes and the crumbled goat's cheese.

3. Drizzle with a little balsamic vinegar and season well with black pepper.

4. Place under a grill for 5–7 minutes until the cheese starts to bubble and the tomatoes soften.

5. Remove and cover with rocket and drizzle with more balsamic.

6. Serve immediately.

Ingredients:

1 wholemeal tortilla

1 tbsp sundried tomato paste

8–12 cherry tomatoes, halved

30–40g goat's cheese, crumbled

Drizzle of balsamic vinegar

Black pepper

Handful of rocket

Nutritional information:

Vegetarian

Chapter 11
Dessert

When attempting a healthy diet or lifestyle choice, we all assume that it is the kiss of death to eat anything naughty and nice, but think again! Desserts have always been the favourite part of my meals and just because you are following a healthy lifestyle does not mean you cannot indulge! Once you have mastered some of the techniques and food swaps used in the following recipes, you will be able to adapt some of your other favourite recipes.

Remember, the quantities given in the recipes are for Xylitol or a sugar alternative. If you are using Stevia, you will need to adjust the quantity indicated to suit your taste as Stevia is very, very sweet and too much can create a more synthetic taste.

Vanilla and Blueberry Brûlée

1. Preheat the oven to 180°C (Gas Mark 4).

2. Take 4 ramekin dishes and place some blueberries in the base of each one.

3. Combine the yoghurt, vanilla paste, egg yolks and cornflour together – I use my hand blender for this. Pour this mixture into the ramekins.

4. Boil the kettle as you need hot water.

5. Choose a deep tray with sides (a roasting tray or Pyrex dish works well) and place the ramekins inside. Then place the tray into the oven. Carefully pour boiling water around the edges of the ramekin dishes until it reaches about halfway up the sides. Bake for 30 minutes.

6. Remove and leave to cool. Once cool, leave them in the fridge for at least 30 minutes before serving.

7. When ready to serve, sprinkle with brown sugar and using a kitchen blow torch, caramelise the tops until they are golden. Alternatively, you can use your grill, but don't walk away as they can brown very very quickly!

8. Serve immediately.

Note: Xylitol does not have the same caramelising properties as sugar so you cannot use it to form the topping.

Ingredients:

150g blueberries
300ml 0% fat natural
   Greek yoghurt
1 tsp vanilla paste
4 egg yolks
1 tbsp cornflour
4 tbsp brown sugar

Nutritional information:

Vegetarian

Fresh Berry Pavlova

Ingredients:

4 egg whites
230g Xylitol
1 tsp cornflour
1 tsp white wine vinegar
300g 0% fat Greek
  yoghurt
3 tbsp low-fat cream
  (optional)
1 tsp vanilla extract
200g berries (I always opt
  for raspberries as they
  are my favourite)
Icing sugar to dust
  (optional)

Nutritional information:

Vegetarian

1. Preheat the oven to 200°C (Gas Mark 6).

2. Place the egg whites in a clean bowl and whisk until glossy and forming soft peaks.

3. Add the Xylitol a little at a time and beat until it forms firm peaks.

4. Mix in the cornflour and vinegar.

5. Line a baking tray with baking parchment. (You can stick the parchment to the tray using a small dollop of the egg white mixture.)

6 Pipe or spoon the mixture onto the parchment to form one large circle of meringue.

7. Place in the oven and immediately lower the temperature to 150°C (Gas Mark 2).

8. Cook for 1 hour and then turn the oven off, leaving the meringue inside to cool. Store in an airtight container until needed.

9. In a bowl mix the yoghurt and cream with the vanilla extract.

10. Place the meringue on a serving plate, add a dollop of the yoghurt mixture and cover with berries.

11. Sprinkle with icing sugar and serve.

Golden Elderflower Jelly

Edible gold glitter

150ml elderflower cordial

450ml sparkling water (or
if you aren't worried
about the calories, you
can use sparkling wine)

4 leaves gelatine (or
vegetarian gelatine)

1–2 handfuls of mixed
berries (e.g. raspberries,
blueberries or red
currants)

Mint leaves

Edible gold leaf (optional
but perfect for a
dramatic dessert)

Nutritional information:

Vegetarian, gluten-free

These look really amazing, especially when served in a beautiful wine or babycham-style glass. Edible glitter and leaf gelatine are available from supermarkets but you may have to go to a specialist kitchen or cake shop for the gold leaf.

1. Place the edible gold glitter in a bowl. Dip the edge of each glass in water (or egg white if you want a really strong 'glue') and then into the glitter. Leave to dry.

2. In a jug, add the cordial and sparking water or wine. Combine well.

3. Place the gelatine leaves in a bowl of cold water and wait until they become flaccid – this takes about 5–8 minutes. Then remove and place in a bowl or cup filled with about 100ml boiling water.

4. Once the gelatine has dissolved, add it to the cordial and sparkling water. Combine well.

5. Pour into your glasses. Add a few of each of the berries to each glass. Place in the fridge until set.

6. Once set, place a few remaining berries in the centre of each of the jellies. Decorate with a few mint leaves and a splattering of gold leaf to create a decadent look.

Ginger, Lemongrass and Lime Jelly

1. In a jug, add the cordial and sparking water. Combine well.

2. Place the gelatine leaves in a bowl of cold water and wait until they become flaccid – this takes about 5–8 minutes. Then remove and place in a bowl or cup filled with about 100ml boiling water. Once the gelatine has dissolved, add it to the cordial and sparkling water. Combine well.

3. Pour into your glasses. Add a few strips of lime peel into each glass. Place in the fridge until set.

Ingredients:

150ml ginger and
  lemongrass cordial
450ml sparkling water (or
  if you aren't worried
  about the calories, you
  can use sparkling wine)
4 leaves gelatine (or
  vegetarian gelatine)
Lime peel

Nutritional information:
Vegetarian, gluten-free

Note: You could also try making jellies with other cordials. For a pink jelly try pomegranate cordial, decorated with a splattering of pomegranate seeds.

Serves

4

Ingredients:

500ml red grape juice

150g Xylitol, Stevia to taste or 4 tbsp Sweet Freedom Dark

1 cinnamon stick (optional)

4 pears, peeled but with the stalks still intact

1 tsp cornflour (optional)

Low-fat ice-cream, low-fat crème fraîche or 0% fat natural Greek yoghurt to serve

Nutritional information:

Vegetarian, vegan, gluten-free

Pink Poached Pears

1. In a saucepan, add the grape juice, your chosen sweetener and the cinnamon stick. Bring slowly to a simmer.

2. Add the peeled pears and poach for 20 minutes, turning them regularly to make sure they are always in the liquid.

3. Remove the cinnamon stick. Place the pears on your serving dishes and drizzle over some of the liquid. If you want to thicken the liquid before drizzling, return the pan to the heat once you have removed the pears. Mix 1 tsp cornflour with a little water in a cup and stir well. Pour this mixture into the saucepan with the grape juice. Bring to the boil and stir constantly until it starts to thicken. Then drizzle over the pears.

4. Serve with a dollop of low fat ice-cream, low fat crème fraîche or 0% fat natural Greek yoghurt.

Gooseberry, Elderflower and Ginger Layer

I love this dessert. It's perfect with fresh gooseberries when in season, but also when made with frozen. You can use standard ginger biscuits, but I prefer low GI Nairn's Stem Ginger Oat Biscuits.

1. Place the gooseberries and the cordial in a pan and simmer gently on a low heat for approximately 10 minutes until the liquid has reduced. Leave to cool.

2. Meanwhile mix the yoghurt, quark and vanilla paste together in a bowl. Leave to one side.

3. Crush the ginger biscuits. You can do this in a food processor or place them in a freezer bag and gently bash with a rolling pin until they are all crushed.

4. When ready, place a little of the gooseberry mixture in the base of each glass or dessert bowl. Top with the yoghurt mixture and finish with the crumbled biscuits.

5. Leave to chill for ½ an hour before serving.

Ingredients:

175g gooseberries, fresh or frozen

350ml elderflower cordial

300ml 0% fat natural Greek yoghurt

125ml quark

1 tsp vanilla paste

120g Nairn's Stem Ginger Oat Biscuits (they are gluten-free)

Nutritional information:

Vegetarian, gluten-free

Raspberry Healthy Brûlée

This is a really yummy dessert that takes minutes to prepare. It looks and tastes far more impressive than it really is and the good news is that it is actually quite healthy!

1. If you are using frozen raspberries, place them in your serving glasses to start defrosting.

2. Meanwhile, mix the yoghurt and crème fraîche together in a bowl. Once combined, add the vanilla paste and stir well.

3. If you are using fresh raspberries, place them now at the bottom of the glasses. Spoon the yoghurt mixture over the raspberries.

4. For an extra healthy topping, instead of the brown sugar, just add a few drizzles of Sweet Freedom Syrup. For those who don't worry about sugar, sprinkle the brown sugar on top of the yoghurt – enough to form a generous layer to make the crème brûlée effect.

5. Using a kitchen blow torch (or your grill – but don't walk away!), caramelise to form a golden layer.

6. Chill before serving. Enjoy!

Note: Xylitol does not have the same caramelising properties as sugar so you cannot use it to form the topping.

Ingredients:

200g fresh or frozen raspberries

350–400g 0% fat Greek yoghurt

3 tbsp low-fat crème fraîche

1 tsp vanilla paste

3–4 tbsp brown sugar or Sweet Freedom Dark

Nutritional information:

Vegetarian, gluten-free

Raspberry Sorbet

Ingredients:

200ml water

1–2 tsp Sweet Freedom Dark

100g Xylitol or Stevia to taste

500g raspberries

Nutritional information:

Vegetarian, vegan, gluten-free

Sorbets are traditionally made with caster sugar and glucose syrup but as I don't want raised blood sugars, I have substituted Xylitol or Stevia. Xylitol will be the favourite if you are like me and don't want an overpowering sweetness. For those who love sugar, you may prefer Stevia – but please, taste the water as you add the Stevia, as it is very sweet and a little goes a long way. You will need to make this sorbet in an ice-cream maker.

1. In a saucepan over a low heat, add the water and the Sweet Freedom Dark. Add either the Xylitol or Stevia a little at a time, tasting the water once dissolved if you want to control the sweetness.

2. Simmer gently until dissolved and it starts to thicken slightly. Then remove and allow to cool completely.

3. Whizz the raspberries in a food processor. If you want a smoother sorbet, then push them through a sieve.

4. When the syrup is cool, blend it with the raspberries.

5. Pour into the ice-cream maker and follow the manufacturer's instructions for making sorbet.

6. Serve with a selection of berries or, for an extra treat, a low GI biscuit.

Berry Cream Meringues

1. Preheat the oven to 200°C (Gas Mark 6).

2. Place the egg whites in a clean bowl and whisk until glossy and forming soft peaks.

3. Add the Xylitol a little at a time and beat until it forms firm peaks.

4. Mix in the cornflour and vinegar.

5. Line a baking tray with baking parchment. (You can stick the parchment to the tray using a small dollop of the egg white mixture.)

6. Pipe or spoon the mixture onto the parchment to form 4–8 small rounds of meringue.

7. Place in the oven and immediately lower the temperature to 150°C (Gas Mark 2).

8. Cook for 1 hour and then turn the oven off, leaving the meringues inside to cool. Store in an airtight container until needed.

9. In a bowl mix the yoghurt with the vanilla extract.

10. Place a meringue on each serving plate, add a dollop of the yoghurt mixture and cover with berries.

11. Sprinkle with icing sugar and serve.

Ingredients:

2 egg whites
115g Xylitol
½ tsp cornflour
½ tsp white wine vinegar
150ml 0% fat Greek
  yoghurt
1 tsp vanilla extract
200g mixed berries
Icing sugar to dust
  (optional)

Nutritional information:

Vegetarian

Healthy Summer Pudding

Ingredients:

800g mixed berries (fresh
    or frozen)
75g Xylitol or Stevia to
    taste
4–6 slices gluten-free
    white bread
Extra berries or icing sugar
    to serve

Nutritional information:

Vegetarian, vegan, gluten-
free

This recipe gives this summer pudding a healthy twist.
Substituting Xylitol or Stevia for sugar reduces raised blood sugar
and swapping white bread for gluten-free is also a healthier
choice. I have tried this using wholemeal bread but gluten-free
white bread gives better results – far more like the original recipe
we all adore.

1. Place the berries in a saucepan and heat gently for 3–4
minutes.

2. Line a basin with cling film, making sure it overlaps the sides
of the bowl so that later you can bring the excess cling film all the
way back over the top to cover the basin. (This helps you remove
the pudding without too many problems.)

3. Line the bowl with the bread slices, overlapping them to
prevent leakage.

4. Then place the berries in the basin. Top with slices of bread
and bring the excess cling film over the top to secure.

5. Press down gently. If the basin is not overfull, you can weigh
the pudding down by placing on top a plate that fits inside the
top of the basin and adding some cans for extra weight.

6. Leave in the fridge overnight or for at least 4–5 hours.

7. To serve, carefully peel back the cling film. Place a serving
plate on the top of the basin, serving side down, then carefully
flip the basin, allowing the pudding to drop onto the plate.

8. You can add more berries before serving or sprinkle with a
little icing sugar.

Simple Baked Apples

This is a delicious and very simple autumnal pudding that always leaves people satisfied.

1. Preheat the oven to 180°C (Gas Mark 4).

2. Wash and core the apples, leaving the skins intact. Place on a baking tray or ovenproof dish.

3. Fill the empty cores with the dried fruit. Finish with a sprinkling of Xylitol or Stevia.

4. Bake in the oven for 25–30 minutes until soft.

5. Serve with low-fat crème fraîche or fat-free natural yoghurt.

Note: In early September, why not make use of the plump ripe blackberries in the hedgerows, and fill the cores with these delicious bulging berries to make Baked Blackberry Apples. Bake these in an ovenproof dish as you will get plenty of sticky juice oozing out from the apples.

Ingredients:

4 Bramley apples

2–3 tbsp raisins or sultanas

2–3 tbsp Xylitol or Stevia to taste

Low-fat crème fraîche or fat-free natural yoghurt to serve

Nutritional information:

Vegetarian, vegan, gluten-free

Ingredients:

300g gooseberries

50g Xylitol, or Stevia to
    taste

250g 0% fat Greek
    yoghurt

Crumbled ginger biscuits
    to serve (optional)

Nutritional information:

Vegetarian, gluten-free

Simple Gooseberry Fool

I love gooseberry fools, but they can be high in fat, especially when made with full-fat cream. Why not try this healthy alternative? Buy your gooseberries in season or grow your own.

1. Place the gooseberries in a pan with the Xylitol or Stevia and gently cook until the gooseberries pop when pushed with a spoon.

2. Leave the gooseberries to cool and then fold in the yoghurt.

3. Place in serving dishes to set. Delicious with ginger biscuit crumbs sprinkled on the top.

Note: You can make Rhubarb Fool by following the same process. If you have a very sweet tooth you may want to add more Xylitol or Stevia.

No-Bake Berry Cheesecake

1. Place the biscuits in a food processor and whizz until you have crumbs. Alternatively, place in a freezer bag and gently bash with a wooden spoon.

2. Place the Pure or margarine in a saucepan and melt for a few minutes over a medium heat. Add the biscuit crumbs and stir well.

3. Place this in a greased loose-bottom flan tin. Push down hard with a spoon to form a firm base. Chill in the fridge to set.

4. Meanwhile, mix the cream cheese, yoghurt, cream, vanilla extract and Xylitol.

5. Place over the biscuit base and smooth. Leave to set in the fridge for a few hours.

6. Just before serving, top the cheesecake with the coulis. Finish with the berries. Serve immediately.

Ingredients:

200g low-fat digestive biscuits

50g Pure or low-fat margarine

300g low-fat cream cheese

150g 0% fat Greek yoghurt

3 tbsp low-fat cream (optional)

2 tsp vanilla essence

25g Xylitol

2–3 tbsp strawberry or raspberry coulis

200g strawberries or raspberries

Nutritional information:

Vegetarian

Baked Ginger Pears

Ingredients:

2–4 pears, peeled, halved
  and cored
Sweet Freedom Dark
1 tsp mixed spice
4–8 ginger biscuits,
  crumbled (I like to use
  low GI Nairn's Stem
  Ginger Oat Biscuits or
  choose gluten-free)
Low-fat crème fraîche to
  serve

Nutritional information:

Vegetarian, vegan, gluten-
free

1. Preheat the oven to 200°C (Gas Mark 6).

2. Place the prepared pears on a baking tray. Drizzle with a small amount of Sweet Freedom – try to keep this within the centre of the pears so it does not escape onto the tray as it may burn.

3. Bake for 10–15 minutes.

4. Meanwhile, crush the ginger biscuits. Place them in a freezer bag and gently bash with a rolling pin.

5. Remove from the oven and drizzle with more Sweet Freedom and a sprinkle of mixed spice. Cover with the crumbled ginger biscuits.

6. Place back in the oven and cook for another 10 minutes or until soft.

7. Serve with a generous dollop of low-fat crème fraîche.

Orange and Rhubarb Betty

Serves
4–6

I adore rhubarb and combined with orange this makes a wonderfully satisfying dessert. A great variation to the standard fruit crumble. If you fancy another variation, why not combine rhubarb and strawberries? Delicious.

1. Preheat the oven to 190°C (Gas Mark 5).

2. Place the rhubarb and orange in a saucepan. Sprinkle with Xylitol or Stevia and add the water. Cook over a medium heat for 5–8 minutes, until the fruit starts to soften but still holds its shape. Stir to help combine flavours.

3. Meanwhile, combine the breadcrumbs, oats and cinnamon powder.

4. Place the fruit in an ovenproof dish and place the crumble mixture over the top.

5. Carefully melt the Pure or margarine and syrup, and pour over the crumble mixture.

6. Place in the oven and cook for 15–20 minutes until the top is golden.

7. Serve with a dollop of low-fat crème fraîche or natural yoghurt.

Ingredients:

750g rhubarb

2 oranges, peeled and chopped

2–3 tbsp Xylitol or Stevia to taste

1–2 tbsp water

150g wholemeal or gluten-free breadcrumbs

100g oats (or gluten-free)

2 tsp cinnamon powder

2 tbsp Pure or low-fat margarine (or vegan)

2 tbsp Sweet Freedom Syrup

Low-fat crème fraîche or natural yoghurt to serve

Nutritional information:

Vegetarian, vegan, gluten-free

Vanilla Panna Cotta

Ingredients:

4 leaves gelatine (or
   vegetarian gelatine)
250ml skimmed milk
2 tsp vanilla extract or
   paste (not artificial
   essence!)
3 tbsp Xylitol or Stevia to
   taste
200g 0% fat Greek
   yoghurt
100g low-fat crème
   fraîche
Fresh fruit or coulis to
   serve

Nutritional information:

Vegetarian, gluten-free

1. Place the gelatine leaves in cold water until they become flaccid.

2. Heat the skimmed milk gently over a low heat until it is just starting to come to a boil.

3. Add the vanilla extract and Xylitol or Stevia. Remember that Stevia is much sweeter so taste to adjust the sweetness.

4. Remove from the heat. Add the gelatine leaves and combine.

5. Leave to cool for about 10 minutes before mixing in the yoghurt and crème fraîche.

6. Pour into ramekin dishes and place in the fridge to set.

7. Serve with some fresh fruit or coulis.

Poached Pomegranate Plums

Pomegranates are rich in antioxidants, vitamins and minerals. Since the fresh fruit is fiddly to eat, many people prefer to use the juice to benefit from the many nutrients this fruit contains.

1. Place the plums in a large saucepan. Add the pomegranate juice, Xylitol, Stevia or Sweet Freedom Syrup with the cinnamon stick and star anise.

2. Bring to the boil gently and then simmer for 5–15 minutes, depending on the ripeness of the plums.

3. Remove the star anise and cinnamon stick.

4. Serve with a dollop of fat-free yoghurt or fat-free ice-cream.

TOP TIP!
Remember that Stevia is very sweet so adjust to taste.

Ingredients:

500g plums, washed, stoned and quartered
200ml pomegranate juice
60g Xylitol (or Stevia to taste, or 2–3 tbsp Sweet Freedom Syrup)
1 cinnamon stick
1 star anise
Fat-free yoghurt or fat-free vanilla ice-cream to serve

Nutritional information:
Vegetarian, vegan, gluten-free

Rhubarb and Custard Pots

500g rhubarb

3–4 tbsp water

1–2 tbsp Xylitol or Stevia
to taste

Custard

450ml skimmed milk

3 tbsp cornflour

3 egg yolks (keep the
whites and use or freeze
them to make
meringues!)

4–5 tbsp Xylitol or Stevia
to taste

1 tsp vanilla extract

Crumbled ginger biscuits
to serve (optional)

Vegetarian

These are seriously yummy and low in fat and sugar, giving you the treat without the guilt factor. Use this recipe to make custard to go with any of your favourite stewed fruit – but remember, when stewing fruit add a little Xylitol or Stevia, not sugar!

1. Place the rhubarb in a pan with the water and the Xylitol or Stevia. Cook gently over a low heat until the rhubarb softens and cooks (5–10 minutes).

2. Meanwhile, place the milk in a saucepan and gently bring to a simmer over a low heat. Do not let it boil over!

3. Meanwhile, mix the cornflour, egg yolks, Xylitol or Stevia and vanilla extract together to form a paste. Remember to use less Stevia as it is very sweet.

4. When the milk starts to simmer, remove from the heat and stir in the paste. Keep stirring until it starts to thicken. You may want to place it back over a low heat (not high or it will burn on the bottom!). Keep stirring until it thickens. If you are unfortunate to get lumps, beat with a balloon whisk, but if you keep it on a low heat and keep stirring you should be fine.

5. Place the rhubarb in the bottom of your serving glasses. Add the custard and finish with a crumble of ginger biscuits or a few more dollops of rhubarb. Serve hot or cold.

Baked Peach and Raspberry Delights

Just like baked apples, this is a very simple dish that tastes wonderful.

1. Preheat the oven to 170°C (Gas Mark 3).

2. Place the halved and stoned peaches in a deep ovenproof tray, flesh facing upwards.

3. In the centre of each halved peach, where the stone was, add ½ tsp Sweet Freedom and top with 2 or 3 raspberries.

4. Sprinkle the flaked almonds over the top of the peaches, retaining a few for later.

5. Bake in the oven for 15 minutes.

6. Meanwhile, mix the yoghurt, quark, Sweet Freedom, orange zest and vanilla essence together.

7. When the peaches are ready, place in serving bowls with a dollop of the yoghurt mixture. Sprinkle with the remaining almonds before serving.

Ingredients:

4 ripe peaches, halved and stoned
4 tsp Sweet Freedom Dark
18–24 raspberries (fresh or frozen)
75g flaked almonds

Topping

100ml fat-free natural yoghurt
100ml quark
1 tsp vanilla essence
Zest of 1 orange
1 tsp Sweet Freedom Syrup

Nutritional information:

Vegetarian

Chapter 12
Sweet treats

One of the things I notice when anyone, including myself, starts on a healthy diet, is our craving for sweet things seems to increase, probably because we know we have to restrain ourselves. I have put together some healthier choices for sweet treats, but that does not mean you can sit and eat a whole cake in one go. Remember, everything in moderation, but if you satisfy a sweet craving with these healthier options you are less likely to go tucking into the biscuit tin or raiding the children's chocolate stash.

Remember, the quantities given in the recipes are for Xylitol or a sugar alternative. If you are using Stevia, you will need to adjust the quantity indicated to suit your taste as Stevia is very, very sweet and too much can create a more synthetic taste.

Fatless Chocolate Sponge

This is a really lovely sponge. It is made without butter and by using Xylitol or Stevia, you don't get the sugar rush. Above all, it tastes great!

1. Preheat the oven to 180°C (Gas Mark 4).

2. Grease two deep sponge tins with butter. Sprinkle on a little flour and ensure the butter is coated. This forms a perfect non-stick base.

3. Whisk the egg yolks and Xylitol or Stevia together, adding the warm water a little at a time. If you are using a mixer, this takes a good 5 minutes, or by hand at least 10 minutes to ensure a light and fluffy texture.

4. Sift the flour and cocoa and gently fold a little at a time into the egg mix – *don't whisk!*

5. Whisk the egg whites until firm, and then very gently fold into the cake mixture.

6. Divide the mixture into the two greased sponge tins. Bake for 15–20 minutes until firm.

7. Place on a cooling rack to cool.

8. Once cool, sandwich with fromage frais. Sprinkle with icing sugar to garnish.

Note: For an extra treat, combine 75g crushed raspberries with the fromage frais –delicious.

Ingredients:
Butter for greasing
4 eggs, separated
225g Xylitol or Stevia to
    taste
75ml warm water
150g self-raising flour (or
    Doves Farm Gluten Free
    Self Raising Flour)
75g good quality cocoa
200g low-fat fromage frais
Icing sugar to sprinkle

Nutritional information:
Vegetarian, gluten-free

Fruity Carrot Cake

3 carrots, grated

200g Xylitol

330ml water

75g dates, chopped

100g raisins or currants

125g Pure or low-fat
    margarine (or vegan)

2 tsp cinnamon

1 tsp ground coriander

500g self-raising flour,
    ideally wholemeal (or
    Doves Farm Gluten Free
    Self Raising Flour)

1 tsp baking powder (or
    gluten-free)

75g walnuts or mixed
    nuts, chopped

Zest of ½ lemon

Mascarpone, Fromage
    Frais and Cinnamon
    Icing (optional)

150g low-fat mascarpone

100g low-fat fromage frais

1 heaped tsp cinnamon

1 rounded tsp Xylitol or
    Stevia to taste

Vegetarian, vegan, gluten-
free

This is a really simple cake to make – it is mostly all done in a saucepan! It is also eggless, making it suitable for vegans if you swap the low-fat margarine for Pure vegan spread. It is also perfect when you have run out of eggs but want a lovely cake. Very moist and delicious, it's worth giving it a go!

1. Place the carrots, Xylitol, water and dried fruit in a saucepan and bring to the boil for about 2–3 minutes.

2. Add the Pure or margarine, cinnamon and ground coriander. Remove from the heat and allow to cool completely (this is very important!).

3. Once completely cooled, preheat your oven to 180°C (Gas Mark 4).

4. Sift in the flour and baking powder. Add the nuts and lemon zest and combine well. It may look a bit of a mess but, believe me, it will be worth it.

5. Place the cake mixture into a lined cake tin (I find cake liners are so easy).

6. Place in the oven and cook for 45–55 minutes. To test, place a clean knife or skewer into the centre of the cake. It must come out clean for the cake to be cooked. Cooking times do vary depending on cookers.

7. Once cooked, turn the cake out onto a cooling rack.

8. Serve as it is or for extra decadence top with icing – I love Mascarpone, Fromage Frais and Cinnamon Icing. Combine all ingredients and beat until fluffy. Cover and chill for at least 1 hour before icing the cake.

Healthy Fruit Cake

I discovered this fruit cake recipe in my great aunt's recipe scrapbook. I don't know where she acquired it, but it is a fatless, sugarless, eggless fruit cake and very simple to make.

1. Preheat the oven to 180°C (Gas Mark 4).

2. Place the dates and tea into a saucepan and gently heat over a medium heat until the dates are soft. Remove the pan from the heat and mash to break up the dates.

3. In a large mixing bowl, sift the flour and baking powder. Add the mixed fruit, orange zest and juice and mix thoroughly.

4. Add the date mixture and stir well.

5. Spoon the mixture into a greased or lined 1kg (2lb) loaf or cake tin. Level the top. If your oven is quite fierce, you may want to place a sheet of greaseproof or brown paper over the top of the cake halfway through cooking to avoid a burnt top.

6. Bake for 45–50 minutes. Reduce the heat to 160°C (Gas Mark 3) and cook for a further 15–30 minutes (until a skewer or knife inserted into the centre of the cake comes out clean).

Ingredients:

200g dates

300ml black tea or water

175g self-raising flour (the health conscious can opt for wholemeal or Doves Farm Gluten Free Self Raising)

1 tsp baking powder (or gluten-free)

Zest and juice of 1 orange

400g dried mixed fruit

1 tbsp orange juice

2 tsp mixed spice

Nutritional information:

Vegetarian, vegan, gluten-free

Ingredients:

4 eggs, beaten

250g Xylitol

2 tsp vanilla extract

200ml very mild/light
olive oil

300g self-raising flour
(ideally wholemeal or
use Doves Farm Gluten
Free Self Raising Flour
and add 30ml water to
the mixture)

1 tsp bicarbonate of soda

2 tsp ground cinnamon

½ tsp nutmeg, grated

400g carrots, grated

50g walnuts or pecan
nuts, chopped

Topping:

Low-fat cream cheese
icing

2 tsp low-fat cream cheese

2 drops vanilla extract

Icing sugar

Chopped nuts or flaked
almonds

Nutritional information:

Vegetarian, gluten-free

Moist Carrot Cake

We all love cake – this carrot cake is not fat free but it's a little healthier than some other recipes. You can decorate this cake with frosted icing, or low-fat cream cheese mixed with icing sugar (see instructions below), or low-fat mascarpone with a little vanilla extract. Alternatively, don't decorate as it keeps longer in an airtight container without icing.

1. Preheat the oven to 180°C (Gas Mark 4).

2. Beat the eggs and Xylitol together until fluffy. Add the vanilla extract and oil and continue to whisk.

3. Sift the flour, bicarbonate of soda, cinnamon and nutmeg together and add gradually to the egg mix.

4. Stir in the carrots and nuts. Mix thoroughly.

5. Place in a greased or lined baking tin (I use a 25cm (10in) cake tin or two sponge tins if sandwiching with icing). Bake in the oven for 45 minutes – 1 hour. Test to see if it is cooked by placing a clean knife or skewer in the centre of the cake. If it comes away clean, the cake is cooked.

6. Place on a cooling rack to cool.

7. If you are icing the cake, mix the low-fat cream cheese and vanilla extract together and keep adding icing sugar until you get a thick, creamy consistency. Decorate with some chopped nuts or flaked almonds.

Did you know?
Walnuts and almonds can help reduce cholesterol.

Lemon Drizzle Cake

This is my son's favourite cake – I have taken a traditional family recipe and substituted low-fat spread and Xylitol. For extra health, use wholemeal flour or Doves Farm Gluten Free Self Raising Flour.

1. Preheat the oven to 190°C (Gas Mark 5) and line your 0.5kg (1lb) loaf tin with a cake liner.

2. In a bowl, beat the Xylitol with the Pure or margarine until it is light and fluffy.

3. Gradually add the eggs, beating as you go.

4. Sift the flour and add this gradually to the mixture, beating well.

5. Add the zest of 2 lemons, the juice of 1 lemon and the lemon essence. Taste the cake mix – if you like a strong lemon flavour, add more zest (not juice as zest gives more flavour).

6. Pour the mixture into the cake tin. Place in the oven and cook for 35–40 minutes, or until a clean knife or skewer inserted into the centre of the cake comes out clean. Leave to cool for 2 minutes.

7. Meanwhile, mix 1–2 tbsp Xylitol with the juice of 1 lemon. You can add some zest if you like the flavour and texture. Carefully drizzle this over the cake while it is still warm. Do not take the cake out of the tin until it has cooled.

8. This cake will keep in an airtight container for 4–5 days.

Ingredients:

225g Xylitol
225g Pure or low-fat margarine
4 eggs, beaten
225g self-raising flour (or wholemeal or Doves Farm Gluten Free Self Raising Flour with 30ml water added to the mixture)
Zest of 2–3 lemons
Juice of 2 lemons
1 tsp lemon essence
1–2 tbsp Xylitol

Nutritional information:

Vegetarian, gluten-free

8–12

depending on size

Ingredients:

225g plain/dark chocolate
    (at least 70% cocoa)
100g Bran Flakes or Fruit
    & Fibre cereal
50g raisins
50g mixed nuts
6–8 apricots, chopped

Nutritional information:

Vegetarian

Chocolate Melts

We used to make these as children. I think it was a ploy of my mum's to try to get some fruit and fibre into us without detection. A good plan, as they are seriously yummy!

1. In a bain marie melt the chocolate. Place a pan of water on your hob and add a heat-proof bowl over the top, making sure the water does not touch the base of the bowl. Over a low/medium heat melt the chocolate.

2. Add the remaining ingredients and stir well.

3. Place dollops on greaseproof paper and leave to set.

Fatless Victoria Sponge

My mum makes a mean fat-less sponge, especially when she uses her homemade raspberry jam to fill it ... yum! I have pinched her recipe to share with you, so go on, and enjoy a guilt-free pleasure! If you use gluten-free flour, add approximately 30ml more water.

1. Preheat the oven to 180°C (Gas Mark 4). Grease two deep sponge tins or use cake liners.

2. Whisk the egg yolks and Xylitol or Stevia together, adding the warm water a little at a time. This normally takes about 10 minutes to ensure a light and fluffy texture.

3. Sift the flour and fold carefully a little at a time into the egg mix – *don't whisk!*

4. Whisk the egg whites until firm, and then very gently fold into the cake mixture.

5. Divide the mixture into the sponge tins. Bake for 15–20 minutes until firm.

6. Place on a cooling rack to cool before filling with raspberry jam.

7. Sprinkle Xylitol, Stevia or icing sugar over to top to complete – delicious!

Ingredients:

3 eggs, separated
225g Xylitol or Stevia
75ml warm water
150g self-raising flour (the health conscious can use wholemeal or Doves Farm Gluten Free)
Raspberry jam filling

Nutritional information:

Vegetarian, gluten-free

Chocolate Popcorn

Ingredients:

75g popping corn
35g dark chocolate (must
  be at least 70% cocoa
  solids), grated
1 heaped tbsp Sweet
  Freedom Dark

Nutritional information:
Vegetarian, vegan

This is a big favourite in our house – the kids can get involved in making it. Remember the chocolate and syrup do add to the calorific value, so if you want a healthier snack, try just plain popcorn – perfect if you are trying to give up crisps and want something to munch.

1. Place the popcorn into your saucepan and add the lid. Place on the hob on a high heat and allow to pop for at least 5 minutes. When the noise stops you know that all the popcorn has popped.

2. Remove from the heat and add the grated chocolate and the syrup. Combine well.

3. Serve immediately.

Did you know?

Dark chocolate does not spike your blood sugar levels like dairy chocolate. As long as you use at least 70% cocoa content, one or two chunks a day has been shown to have health benefits due to high antioxidant content.

Blackcurrant and Apple Bran Loaf

Makes
6–8
slices

In the early eighties my mum was keen to install as much fibre in our diets as possible. She sent away for a booklet of recipes from Kellogg's® All-Bran, which became a bit of a bible for her. Years later we are still making some of the recipes. This is one of our favourites, which we have adapted over the years.

1. Preheat the oven to 180°C (Gas Mark 4).

2. Beat the Xylitol and Pure or margarine together until light and fluffy. Gradually add the eggs and yoghurt and continue to whisk.

3. Add the bran and gradually fold in the sifted flour. Stir well.

4. Finally add the nuts, apple and blackcurrants. When thoroughly mixed, place in a 1kg (2lb) greased or lined loaf tin.

5. Bake for 40 minutes. Leave in the tin for 10 minutes before turning out onto a cooling rack.

6. This is delicious hot as a pudding served with yoghurt or low-fat crème fraîche, or leave to cool and slice.

Ingredients:

75g Xylitol

100g Pure or low-fat margarine

2 eggs, beaten

150g low-fat yoghurt

75g All-Bran

150g self-raising flour (or wholemeal if you want an extra healthy loaf), sifted

100g nuts, finely chopped (hazelnuts or mixed nuts)

1 large cooking apple, chopped

125g blackcurrants (fresh or frozen)

Nutritional information:

Vegetarian

Ingredients:

225g self–raising flour (or
   self-raising wholemeal,
   or Doves Farm Gluten
   Free Self Raising with
   30ml of skimmed milk
   added)
½ tsp baking powder (or
   gluten-free)
25g Xylitol
50g Pure or low-fat
   margarine
100g blueberries
150ml natural yoghurt or
   buttermilk
1 tsp vanilla essence
A little milk or beaten egg

Nutritional information:
Vegetarian, gluten-free

Blueberry Scones

1. Preheat the oven to 200°C (Gas Mark 6).

2. Sift the flour and baking powder into a bowl and add the Xylitol. Combine.

3. Rub the Pure or margarine into the flour until it resembles breadcrumbs.

4. Add the blueberries, yoghurt or buttermilk and vanilla essence and mix.

5. Place the dough on a floured surface and roll into a thick sausage. Cut 2.5–5cm pieces and place these flat onto a greased or lined baking tray.

6. Coat with a little milk or beaten egg before placing in the oven for 12–15 minutes

Chapter 13
Weekly menu plans

Menu plans really do help you to save money and also help prevent you coming home and wondering what to cook. You don't necessarily need to follow my suggestions. Simply pick out some recipes and pop them on a weekly menu plan – create about four or five of these and you can then mix and match as you go. Remember that you can create shopping lists using these plans, which will save you time and money.

Suggested snacks

Fruit and vegetables	Unlimited. Why not chop some vegetables into sticks or make some fruit kebabs?
Natural fat-free yoghurt	I am a big fan of natural yoghurt for cooking and as a snack. Add some fresh fruit, nuts and seeds and you have an indulgent yet healthy snack.
Low GI Nairn's Oatcakes	I am a big fan! They are gluten-free and low GL.
Nuts and seeds	Yes the 'experts' will tell you they are high in fat, but it is a good fat so please enjoy. But, as with anything, don't over load.
Sprouted pulses	You can buy these from whole food shops or sprout your own. Full of nutrients, they add a nutty extra to a salad or even a sandwich. They will also help fill you up.
Dark chocolate	Make sure it really is dark chocolate (not milk!). It should contain at least 70% cocoa. Eat one or two squares a day – this might not sound like much but the taste will explode in your mouth and, in this case, less is more!
Fruit and vegetable juices or homemade smoothies	Some shop-bought smoothies can contain unwanted extras.

Monday

Breakfast	Porridge with Fresh Fruit
Mid-morning snack	Apple Munchies
Lunch	Tomato and Chilli Soup with wholemeal or rye bread and Hummus Slice of Moist Carrot Cake
Mid-afternoon snack	2 Nairn's Oatcakes
Dinner	Quorn Bolognaise Stuffed Tomatoes with Savoury Rice Salad Raspberry Healthy Brûlée

Tuesday

Breakfast	Boiled Egg with wholemeal or rye soldiers
Mid-morning snack	Fresh fruit
Lunch	Wild Rice and Lentil Salad with Salsa Blueberry Scone
Mid-afternoon snack	Vegetable sticks and Hummus
Dinner	Baked Salmon with New Potato Salad and Yoghurt Dressing Rhubarb and Custard Pots

Wednesday

Breakfast	Garlic and Thyme Grilled tomatoes with 2 slices of lean ham
Mid-morning snack	Frank Flu Zapper Juice
Lunch	Smoked Cream of Split Pea Soup with rye bread Fresh fruit
Mid-afternoon snack	Chocolate Melts
Dinner	Tuscan-style Chicken Ginger, Lemongrass and Lime Jelly

Thursday

Breakfast	Tofu Scrambled Eggs with rye bread
Mid-morning snack	Blue Moon Juice
Lunch	Lentil Dahl Lemon Drizzle Cake
Mid-afternoon snack	2 Nairn's Oatcakes
Dinner	Lemon and Ginger Mackerel Salad No Bake Berry Cheesecake

Friday

Breakfast	Porridge with Spicy Fruit Compote
Mid-morning snack	2 Nairn's Oatcakes and fresh fruit
Lunch	Roasted Pumpkin Soup Fatless Victoria Sponge
Mid-afternoon snack	Vegetable sticks and Hummus
Dinner	Baked Coley, Fennel and Red Onion with steamed new potatoes and a fresh green salad Vanilla Panna Cotta

Saturday

Breakfast	Mackerel Pâté with rye bread
Mid-morning snack	Smooth Operator Smoothie
Lunch	Pear and Celeriac Soup Simple Gooseberry Fool
Mid-afternoon snack	Chocolate Popcorn
Dinner	Quorn Meatball Hotpot Poached Pomegranate Plums

Sunday

Breakfast	Tofu Scrambled Eggs with 2 slices of lean ham and grilled tomatoes
Mid-morning snack	Fresh fruit
Lunch	Rainbow Bean and Feta Salad Slice of Fatless Chocolate and Raspberry Sponge
Mid-afternoon snack	Blue Moon Juice
Dinner	Lamb, Chickpea and Apricot Casserole Vanilla and Blueberry Brûlée

Index